SCHOOLHOUSE

◇

QUILTS

Edited by
Karen Costello Soltys

 Rodale Press, Emmaus, Pennsylvania

Editor: *Karen Costello Soltys*
Technical Editor: *Karen Bolesta*
Technical Writer: *Darra Duffy Williamson*
Quilt Scout: *Bettina Havig*
Cover and Interior Designer: *Denise M. Shade*
Book Layout: *Nancy J. Smola*
Photographer: *Mitch Mandel*
Illustrator: *Sandy Freeman*
Studio Manager: *Leslie Keefe*
Copy Editor: *Carolyn Mandarano*
Editorial Assistance: *Stephanie Wenner*
Manufacturing Coordinator: *Jodi Schaffer*

RODALE HOME AND GARDEN BOOKS

Vice President and Editorial Director:
Margaret J. Lydic
Managing Editor, Quilt Books: *Suzanne Nelson*
Art Director: *Michael Mandarano*
Associate Art Director: *Mary Ellen Fanelli*
Copy Director: *Dolores Plikaitis*
Office Manager: *Karen Earl-Braymer*

We're happy to hear from you.
If you have any questions or comments concerning
the editorial content of this book, please write to:
Rodale Press, Inc.
Book Readers' Service
33 East Minor Street
Emmaus, PA 18098
For more information about Rodale Press and the
books and magazines we publish, visit our World
Wide Web site at:
http://www.rodalepress.com

The quilt shown on pages 112 and 113 is owned by
Doris Adomsky of Ivyland, Pennsylvania.

ISBN 0–87596–975–5 paperback
**The Library of Congress has cataloged the hard-
cover edition as follows:**
The Classic American quilt collection.
Schoolhouse /
  edited by Karen Costello Soltys.
    p. cm.
  ISBN 0–87596–685–3 (hardcover : alk. paper)
  1. Quilting—Patterns. 2. Patchwork—Patterns.
3. School buildings in art. I. Soltys, Karen
Costello.
TT835.C5928   1995
746.46—dc20   95–35249

Distributed in the book trade by St. Martin's Press

2 4 6 8 10 9 7 5 3 1   paperback

CONTENTS

ACKNOWLEDGMENTS

Antique Indigo Schoolhouses, made by Sally Tanner, Tampa, Florida. Sally drafted her Schoolhouse quilt as a way to use a box of old blue scrap fabrics. It has been exhibited in the Third Continental Quilting Congresss in Tampa, the World of Quilts in Rochester, Michigan, and in the Florida Keys Quilters show. This quilt was also featured in the September 1983 issue of *Quilters Newsletter Magazine.* Sally is a charter member of Quilters Workshop of Tampa Bay, as well as the founder of the Florida Keys Quilters Guild.

The Eclectic Neighborhood, made by Margaret Harrison, Charleston, South Carolina. Margaret began this unusual exploration of color and motion in Mary Golden's housing development class. It won second place in the pieced wallhanging category in the Charleston Cobblestone Quilters Guild 1994 show. Margaret is a member of that guild as well as a member of the newly formed Quilters of South Carolina.

Homespun Houses, made by Gerry Sweem, Reseda, California. Gerry is an award-winning quilter with ribbons from AIQA shows in Houston and the Lancaster Quilter's Heritage Celebration. Several of her quilts have also been published in quilting magazines. She is an avid hand quilter who, according to her husband, eats, sleeps, breathes, and quilts. Gerry is a member of the Valley Quiltmakers Guild and San Fernando Valley Quilt Guild.

All-American Schoolhouses, made by Sharyn Craig, El Cajon, California. Sharyn is a nationally recognized quilting teacher and author. As a teacher, she admits that the Schoolhouse block is a sentimental favorite of hers. She combined traditional schoolhouses with pieced stars in this project to use as a class sample on quilt settings.

Little Red Schoolhouses, made by Mary Stori, Prospect Heights, Illinois. Mary is a nationally recognized quilter, teacher, and author whose quilts have won numerous awards, including Best of Show in the 1993 AQS/Hobbs Fashion Show and First Place in the 1991 National Quilt Festival/Silver Dollar City show. Although she is best known for her one-of-a-kind quilts and wearable art, Mary began as a traditional quilter and loves old two-color quilts.

Row Houses, made by Judy Spahn, Clifton, Virginia. Judy's quiltmaking career includes teaching seminars and publishing her quilts in books and magazines. Her unusual Rowhouse setting was a design experiment, her favorite part of quiltmaking. Judy has been a staff member of Jinny Beyer's Hilton Head seminar for 12 years, as well as a member of an art group, New Image. Both of these experiences have provided creative stimulation for her quiltmaking.

House Medallion, made by Susan Loveless Bengston, Rising Sun, Indiana. Susan is an active member of several quilt guilds and groups. Her love of quilting has prompted her to take classes, teach classes, work in quilt shops, and enter quilt shows, where she has won a number of ribbons.

My Cabin Made of Logs, made by Jane Graff, Delafield, Wisconson. Jane has been quilting for 12 years and competes on local, state, and national levels. She also teaches and lectures on quiltmaking. Her Schoolhouse quilt was juried in the 1994 American Quilter's Society show, and won First Prize in the pieced category as well as the Judges Recognition Award at the 1994 Wisconsin State Fair. Jane is a fabric collector and confesses that for this queen-size quilt, she only had to purchase the backing fabric— the rest was already part of her collection!

Honeymoon Cottage, owned by Cindy Rennels, Clinton, Oklahoma. Cindy is an antique quilt dealer and the proprietor of Cindy's Quilts. The Honeymoon Cottage is a traditional 1930s variation of the Schoolhouse pattern, and this particular example was machine pieced and hand quilted in Florida in the 1930s or 1940s.

Memories of SS#3, made by Doreen Hugill, Mount Elgin, Ontario, Canada. Doreen made this quilt as a commissioned project, yet the design was based on her memories of her primary school.

Teacher of the Year, made by Miriam Dean, Winston-Salem, North Carolina. Miriam's inspiration for this quilt began with the bell tower of the small country church of which she is a member. Her original block and quilting designs have garnered several awards for this charming quilt. Teacher of the Year was also featured in the Fall 1990 issue of *Quilt* magazine. Miriam has been quilting since 1981, and she primarily makes quilts for her family, friends, and charitable organizations.

INTRODUCTION

✦

*Quilt names endowed a hand crafted piece of needlework with personal meaning
and were inspired by a wide range of experiences. Religion, domestic life, the community...
were all reflected in expressive and often lyrical pattern names. Significant buildings
such as churches, schoolhouses, and log cabins were stitched
into a host of figurative patterns.*

—Susan Jenkins, *The American Quilt Story*

As I began my search for Schoolhouse quilts to feature in this book, I had a nagging worry. What if I couldn't find enough variations that looked different? What if they all began to look alike? My nightmare was that I'd end up with a book filled with little red houses on white backgrounds.

As I was pondering my dilemma, I took a drive around my hometown, nestled in the gently rolling hills of eastern Pennsylvania. I noticed the little red brick schoolhouse with a white cupola that is now a candy and confections shop. I pass by that schoolhouse every week, but now for the first time I wondered if it had ever been the inspiration for a Schoolhouse quilt in the hundred or so years it has been standing. The idea intrigued me, and I started thinking about other schoolhouses in the area. There was the two-story schoolhouse with a bell tower where my older sister attended first grade. And how could I forget the part-log schoolhouse in the next town, which now is a delightfully quaint country home? I was amazed when I realized just how different the three schoolhouses in my little corner of the world are from each other. I began to see that there could be a lot of room for "architectural differences" in Schoolhouse quilts, too.

After lots of phone calls and searching across the country, I'm pleased to say that's just what this volume offers—architectural variety! As you flip through the pages of this book, you will discover a wide range of Schoolhouse blocks. These patterns vary greatly not only in terms of the style, shape, and size of the overall block but also in the image of the house as well. In some, the house evokes the nostalgia of a rural one-room schoolhouse. In others, the proportions suggest the simplified lines of

the humble, hand-hewn log cabin. One variation conjures the romantic feel of a vine-covered honeymoon cottage, while yet another sports the sleek, contemporary look of the newest house in the neighborhood.

Most quilt historians agree that the earliest examples of what we commonly call the Schoolhouse or House block appeared sometime in the late 1800s, probably sometime after 1870. According to Barbara Brackman in her landmark book *Clues in the Calico: A Guide to Identifying and Dating Antique Quilts*, early House blocks were identified by a variety of names, including Log Cabin, Old Kentucky Home, Old Folks at Home, and Lincoln Log Cabin. It was Ruth Finley who first used the name Little Red Schoolhouse in her 1929 book *Old Patchwork Quilts and the Women Who Made Them*.

Seventy years later, the Schoolhouse block still works its special charm on quiltmakers. No matter whether you live in a rural setting, as I do, where tiny schoolhouses dot the hillsides, or in a thoroughly modern city where high-rise schools are commonplace, I'm sure you'll fall in love with more than one of the Schoolhouse quilts in this volume. And I hope this collection of quilts will open your eyes as much as it did mine to the unlimited design possibilities one simple truly American quilt block can yield.

Karen Soltys

Karen Costello Soltys

SCHOOLHOUSE
PROJECTS

ANTIQUE INDIGO SCHOOLHOUSES

Skill Level: *Intermediate*

A cherished collection of vintage blue fabric takes center stage in this spiffy version of the Schoolhouse pattern, made by Sally Tanner. The country-fresh color scheme creates a clean, crisp image and is an ideal choice for this classic mix of piecework and appliqué. A simple but stunning ribbon border on this twin-size quilt provides the perfect complement.

BEFORE YOU BEGIN

The instructions for this quilt are written based on quick-cutting techniques. With the exception of a few simple shapes that require templates, most of the pieces can be rotary cut. Fabrics can be layered for even more efficient cutting.

Like the other Schoolhouse blocks in this book, the pieced blocks in this quilt are perfect for machine work. There is one basic difference: In this variation, the window sashes are appliquéd in place. The "Sew Easy" box on page 6 offers tips for making the neat, narrow fabric strips ideally suited for this purpose.

Read through "Schoolhouse Basics," beginning on page 104, before you begin this quilt. In addition to specific instructions concerning use of the rotary cutter, you'll find information and hints designed to help in the construction of the basic Schoolhouse block.

CHOOSING FABRICS

Here is the perfect opportunity to use up bits and scraps of those sentimental fabrics you've been saving for an extra-special project. In fact, the quiltmaker choose this particular variation of the Schoolhouse block and designed the wonderfully scrappy pieced border to make use of the smallest, precious bits of her prized antique fabrics. Blues can range from royal to Williamsburg, navy to powder—or anything in between.

You might choose to make all of the houses from the same blue fabric or mix and match as this quiltmaker has done. She pieced each Schoolhouse block from its own blue print, but you can combine different blue fabrics in a single block to make the best use of the material on hand.

Quilt Sizes		
	Twin (shown)	Double
Finished Quilt Size	64½" × 76½"	76½" × 88½"
Finished Block Size	10"	10"
Number of Blocks	20	30

Materials		
	Twin	Double
Muslin	2⅞ yards	4 yards
Assorted blue print scraps	2 yards	3 yards
Navy print	1⅞ yards	2 yards
Ecru with navy dots	⅓ yard	⅜ yard
Backing	4 yards	5⅓ yards
Batting	73" × 85"	85" × 97"

NOTE: Yardages are based on 44/45-inch-wide fabrics that are at least 42 inches wide after preshrinking.

3

Cutting Chart

Fabric	Used For	Strip Width	Number of Strips Twin	Number of Strips Double	Second Cut Dimensions	Number to Cut Twin	Number to Cut Double
Navy	Border 4	4½"	8	9			
Muslin	Border 1	2½"	7	9			
	Border 3	2½"	8	9			
	Sashing	2½"	10	15			
	E	5"	1	2	2" × 5"	20	30
	H	1½"	3	4	1½" × 4½"	20	30
	K	1"	3	5	1" × 6¼"	20	30
	L	1¾"	4	5	1¾" × 3½"	40	60
	P	1¼"	4	5	1¼" × 6½"	20	30

Fabric	Used For	Piece or Dimensions	Number to Cut per House
Each blue print	A	Template A	1
	C	Template C	1
	F	1½" × 2"	2
	G	1¾" × 4½"	2
	I	1" × 4"	1
	J	1¾" × 4"	1
	M	1½" × 3½"	1
	N	1½" × 4"	2
	O	1¾" × 5½"	2
	Window sashing	⅞" × 10½"	1
Muslin	B	Template B	1
	D	Template D	1
	D reverse	Template D	1

Fabric	Used For	Piece	Number to Cut Twin	Number to Cut Double
Ecru with navy dots	X	Template X	72	88
Blue prints	Y	Template Y	36	44
	Y reverse	Template Y	36	44
	Z	Template Z	4	4

Should blue not be your cup of tea, any other two-color scheme would be equally attractive. For the true free spirit, a total scrap bag approach would be handsome as well.

To develop your own color scheme for the quilt, photocopy the **Color Plan** on page 11, and use crayons or colored pencils to experiment with different color arrangements.

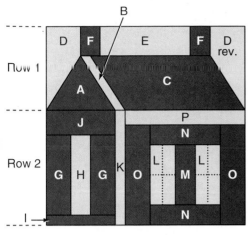

Cut sizes
E = 2" × 5"
F = 1½" × 2"
G = 1¾" × 4½"
H = 1½" × 4½"
I = 1" × 4"
J = 1¾" × 4"
K = 1" × 6¼"
L = 1¾" × 3½"
M = 1½" × 3½"
N = 1½" × 4"
O = 1¾" × 5½"
P = 1¼" × 6½"

Block Diagram

CUTTING

All measurements include ¼-inch seam allowances. Refer to the Cutting Chart and cut the required number of pieces or strips in the sizes needed. Cut all strips across the fabric width (crosswise grain).

For ease of construction, rotary-cutting dimensions, as well as a letter identification, are given for each pattern piece in the **Block Diagram** that is rotary cut. For example, the piece labeled G, which is 1¾ × 4½ inches, does not require a template to cut. The letter label is simply given for easy reference. Because some of the pieces are very similar but not identical, it will be helpful for you to label your stacks of pieces by their letters.

Make templates for pieces A, B, C, D, X, Y, and Z using the full-size pattern pieces on pages 12–13. Refer to page 116 for complete details on making and using templates. The Cutting Chart indicates how many of each piece to cut with each template. Place the B, C, Y, and Z templates wrong side up on the fabric to cut pieces B, C, Y, and Z. Turn the Y template over to cut Y reverse pieces. Reserve a 27-inch square of navy fabric for bias binding.

Note: Cut and piece one sample block before cutting all the fabric for the quilt. You may also want to piece together a few of the ribbon border pieces to test your templates for accuracy before cutting all of the X, Y, and Z pieces.

PIECING THE SCHOOLHOUSE BLOCKS

Refer to the **Block Diagram** as you assemble each block. Note that all of the house pieces for a single block are cut from the same blue fabric. You may find it helpful to lay out all the pieces for one block before stitching any of the units together.

Step 1. Sew an A, B, and C piece together in sequence, as shown in **Diagram 1**. Press the seams toward B.

Diagram 1

Step 2. Sew a blue F chimney to either side of a muslin E strip, as shown in **Diagram 2**. Press the seams toward the chimneys. Stitch this pieced strip to the top edge of the roof, as shown. Press the seams as desired.

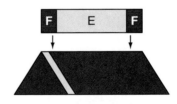

Diagram 2

Step 3. Set in the muslin D and D reverse pieces, as shown in **Diagram 3**. For D, begin stitching ¼ inch from the raw edge at the point where the A, B, and F pieces meet. For D reverse, begin stitching ¼ inch from the raw edge at the point where C and F meet. In each case, stitch outward in the direction indicated by the arrows.

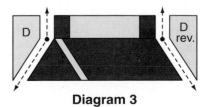

Diagram 3

Press the seams away from the D pieces. Refer to page 109 for additional information on pivoted, or set-in, seams. This completes Row 1. Set aside.

Step 4. For the front of the house, sew a blue G piece to either side of a muslin H piece along their longest sides, as shown in **Diagram 4**. Press the seams toward the blue pieces.

Diagram 4

Step 5. Add a blue I piece along the bottom edge and a blue J piece along the top edge of the house front, as shown in **Diagram 5**. In each case, press the seam toward the newly added piece.

Complete the house front by adding a muslin K piece along the right edge, as shown. Press the seam away from the K piece. Set the completed unit aside.

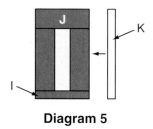

Diagram 5

Step 6. The window sashing is appliquéd to the muslin L pieces before the windows are pieced into the Schoolhouse block. Refer to the "Sew Easy" for tips on making the appliqué window sashing strips. Use the ⁷⁄₈ × 10¹⁄₂-inch strips cut and set aside for this purpose to make window sashings that finish about ³⁄₈ inch wide. Cut each finished sashing strip into two 3¹⁄₂-inch-long segments and two 1³⁄₄-inch-long segments.

Step 7. Finger press the L pieces lengthwise and crosswise to mark both the horizontal and vertical midpoints, as shown in **Diagram 6A**. Center a 1³⁄₄-inch-long window sashing strip over

the crosswise crease on an L piece and use your preferred method of appliqué to stitch the strip in place. Repeat to stitch a 3¹⁄₂-inch-long strip in position over the lengthwise crease, as shown in **6B**. Repeat to make the second window block.

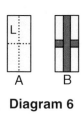

Diagram 6

Sew Easy

Bias bars, ideal for making narrow bias strips, are useful when making straight-grain strips, too, which means they're perfect for making the window sashing in this quilt.

To use the bars, fold and press the cut strip with *wrong* sides together, aligning the lengthwise raw edges. Use your sewing machine to take a ¹⁄₈-inch seam along the raw edge.

Run the appropriate size rod into the tunnel created by the seam. Adjust the strip so that the seam is centered over one flat side of the rod and press the seam allowance to one side. Use a touch of spray starch for a nice, crisp finish. Remove the rod carefully; if it's metal, it may be hot!

Place the finished strip, seam allowance down, on the quilt block. Pin or baste in place, and you're ready to appliqué.

Step 8. Sew an appliquéd L piece to either side of a blue M piece, as shown in **Diagram 7**. Press the seams toward the blue fabric. Add an N piece along the top and bottom edges of this new unit, as shown. In each case, press the seams toward the newly added piece.

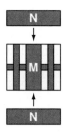

Diagram 7

Step 9. Stitch a blue O piece to the left and right sides of the window unit, as shown in **Diagram 8**. Press the seams toward the newly added pieces. Complete the side of the house by adding a muslin P strip along the top edge of the unit. Press the seam away from P.

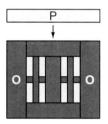

Diagram 8

Step 10. Join the two completed units, as shown in **Diagram 9**, to complete Row 2. Press the seam toward the side of the house. Then, referring to the **Block Diagram** on page 5, sew Rows 1 and 2 together to complete the Schoolhouse block, carefully matching the seams where the roof and house meet. Press the seam in either direction.

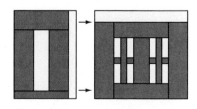

Diagram 9

Step 11. Repeat Steps 1 through 10 to make 20 blocks for the twin-size quilt or 30 blocks for the double-size quilt.

ASSEMBLING THE QUILT TOP

Step 1. From the 2½-inch-wide muslin sashing strips, cut 10½-inch-long pieces for horizontal sashes. You will need 16 pieces for the twin-size quilt and 25 pieces for the double-size quilt.

Step 2. Regardless of the size quilt you are making, you will need to piece the vertical sashing strips to achieve the necessary length. Join the remaining 2½-inch-wide muslin strips in pairs. For the twin size, you will need three long vertical sashing strips; for the double size, you will need four. Trim these long pieced strips to fit your vertical rows, which should be 58½ inches for the twin-size quilt and 70½ inches for the double-size quilt.

Step 3. Refer to the **Twin-Size Assembly Diagram** and use a design wall or other flat surface to lay out the Schoolhouse blocks and the sashing strips in vertical rows. The twin-size quilt will have four vertical rows of five blocks each, separated by short horizontal sashing strips, as shown. The double-size quilt will have five vertical rows of six blocks each, separated by sashing strips. Sew the Schoolhouse blocks and horizontal sashing strips

Twin-Size Assembly Diagram

together in rows, as shown on page 7. Press the seams toward the Schoolhouse blocks.

Step 4. Join the rows and the vertical sashing strips, taking care to align blocks horizontally before pinning and stitching. Ease as necessary for a proper fit. Press seams away from the sashing.

ADDING THE MITERED BORDERS

The quilt shown has a series of four borders. Two are muslin, one is pieced, and the outer border is a blue print. All borders are mitered.

Step 1. For the first muslin border, the strips need to be pieced. For the twin size, sew two $2\frac{1}{2}$-inch-wide muslin strips together with a diagonal seam for a side border, and press the seams as desired. Make another long border strip in the same manner and trim both strips to the length of your quilt top plus two times the border width plus 5 inches for mitering. For the top and bottom borders, cut one of the remaining $2\frac{1}{2}$-inch-wide muslin strips in half, and sew one half to each of the remaining two strips. Press the seams. Trim the borders to the width of your quilt top plus two times the border width plus 5 inches, as for the side borders.

For the double size, sew the $2\frac{1}{2}$-inch-wide muslin border strips together in pairs to make four long strips. Measure the width of quilt top through the center, and add two times the border width plus 5 inches to the total. Trim two strips to this length for the top and bottom borders. Cut the remaining $2\frac{1}{2}$-inch muslin strip in half, and sew one half to each of the remaining long strips. Measure the length of the quilt through the center, and add two times the border width plus 5 inches. Trim the strips to this length for the top and bottom borders.

Step 2. Fold a side border in half crosswise and crease. Unfold it and position it right side down along one side of the quilt top, with the crease at the quilt's midpoint. Pin and sew the border in place, using a $\frac{1}{4}$-inch seam allowance. Begin and end sewing $\frac{1}{4}$ inch from the raw edge of the quilt

top. Repeat on the opposite side. Do not trim the border even with the edges of the top and bottom of the quilt top.

Step 3. Repeat the process described in Step 2 to attach the top and bottom borders to the quilt top. Finish the border by mitering the corners, referring to page 119 for complete instructions.

Assembling the Pieced Border

Step 1. Sew an ecru print X triangle to either side of a blue Z piece, as shown in **Diagram 10**. Press the seams toward Z. Make four of these units and set them aside.

Diagram 10

Step 2. Sew a blue print Y and Y reverse piece to either side of an ecru print X, as shown in **Diagram 11**. Press the seams away from X. For the twin quilt, make a total of 36 such units; for the double quilt, make a total of 44.

Diagram 11

Step 3. Join the Y/X/Y reverse units into strips, using an ecru X piece to link the units, as shown in **Diagram 12**. For the twin-size quilt, make four strips of four units each for the top and bottom borders, and four strips of five units each for the side borders. For the double quilt, make a total of four strips of five units each and four strips of six units each.

Diagram 12

Step 4. Referring to **Diagram 13**, sew a long, Y/X/Y reverse strip to each side of a previously

Diagram 13

pieced X/Z/X unit. Be sure each of the long strips is the same length. Press the seams away from the X pieces. Make four of these long border units. Note that each finished border strip has a Y piece at one end and a Y reverse piece at the other end, so each border is already angled for mitering.

Step 5. Referring to the **Quilt Diagram** on page 10, sew one of the longer pieced border strips to each side of the quilt top. The strip should be positioned so that the narrowest exposed side of piece Z is closest to the center of the quilt. Since the corners will be mitered, begin and end sewing

········Sew Quick········

When attaching long sashing strips between rows of blocks, it can be tricky aligning the blocks from row to row. Here's a quick and easy way to mark the points for matching on the sashing strips.

Layer a couple of strips (as many as you can snip through with your scissors), then use your rotary ruler to measure the distance from one block to the next. For instance, in this quilt, the finished blocks are 10 inches square. First measure ¼ inch from one end of the strips (for the seam allowance) and make a small snip at the edge of the sashing strip. Measure 10 inches from the first snip and make another small cut in the sashing strips. Measure the finished width of the horizontal sashing strips (2 inches in this case) and snip again. Continue measuring the 10 inches then 2 inches and making snips. Repeat for the other side of the strips, then pin the strips to the rows of quilt blocks, matching the snips with the seam intersections.

¼ inch from the raw edge as these border strips are added.

Step 6. In a similar manner, sew the shorter pieced border strips to the top and bottom edges of the quilt top.

Step 7. Complete the border by sewing the angled seams to join the Y and Y reverse pieces in each corner.

Adding the Outer Borders

Step 1. Both the outer muslin and navy print borders must be pieced in the manner described in Step 1 of "Adding the Mitered Borders" to achieve the proper lengths. For the twin-size quilt, you can simply join pairs of like-color border strips for each side of the quilt. For the double size, the top and bottom borders are made by joining two strips, but the side borders each require two and a half strips. To determine the length needed for the borders, measure the quilt through the vertical and horizontal center. Add 5 inches to each length for mitering. Trim all borders to the lengths you calculated.

Step 2. Sew a side muslin border to the corresponding navy border to make a border unit. Press the seam toward the navy strip. Make two of these border units. Sew the top and bottom muslin borders to the top and bottom navy borders in the same manner.

Step 3. Referring to the **Quilt Diagram**, position each border unit so that the muslin strip is closest to the center of the quilt and the blue strip is on the outside. Sew the border strips to the edges of the quilt top. Be sure to start and stop sewing ¼ inch from each end of the quilt top.

Step 4. Miter the corner seams, mitering both borders in one step. Refer to page 119 for more details on mitering borders.

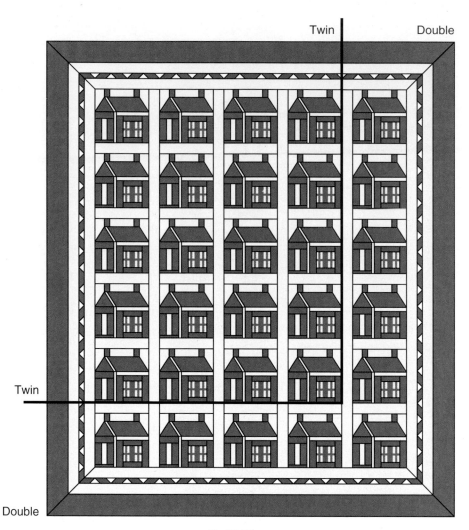

Quilt Diagram

QUILTING AND FINISHING

Step 1. Mark the quilt top for quilting. In the quilt shown, each Schoolhouse block is outline quilted, with additional diagonal line quilting in the roof of each house. The pieced border is quilted in the ditch. The sashing and the unpieced borders are quilted in a diamond pattern.

Step 2. Regardless of which size quilt you've chosen to make, you'll need to piece the backing. For either quilt, cut the backing fabric in half crosswise, and trim the selvages. Cut one piece in half lengthwise, and sew one half to each side of the full-width piece. Press the seams away from the center panel. For the twin size, the seams will

run parallel to the top and bottom of the quilt. For the double size, the seams will run parallel to the sides of the quilt. Refer to page 111 for more information on pieced backings.

Step 3. Layer the backing, batting, and quilt top, and baste the layers together.

Step 4. Quilt all marked designs, adding any additional quilting as desired.

Step 5. Referring to the directions on page 121, make and attach double-fold bias binding. Use the square of navy print fabric that has been set aside for this purpose. For the twin size, you will need about 292 inches of double-fold bias; for the double size, you will need about 340 inches.

ANTIQUE INDIGO SCHOOLHOUSES

Color Plan

Photocopy this page and use it to experiment with color schemes for your quilt.

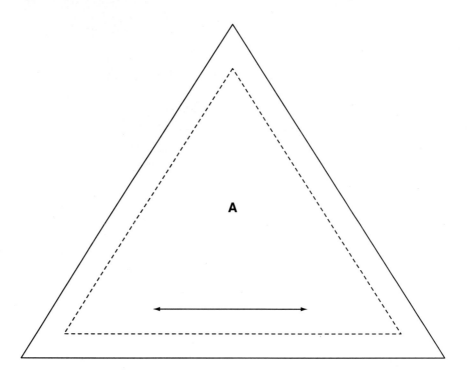

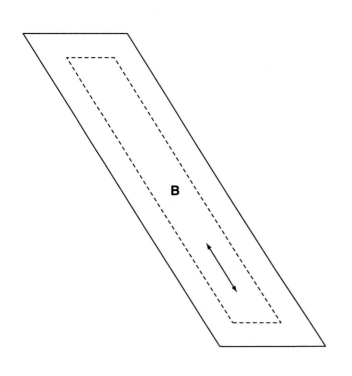

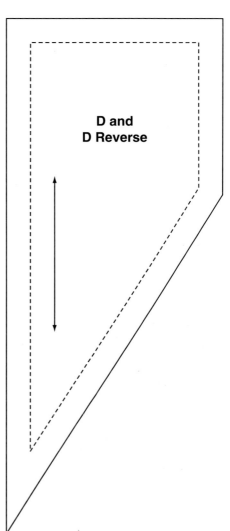

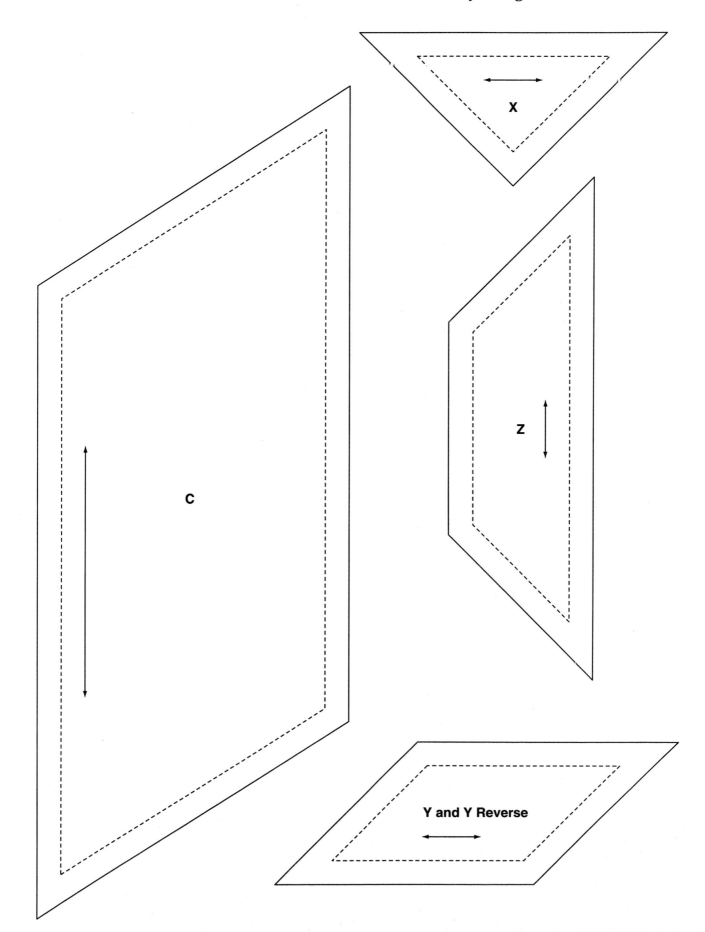

The Eclectic Neighborhood

Skill Level: *Challenging*

I *nspired by a workshop with Mary Golden, quiltmaker Margaret*
Harrison put a new spin on a familiar pattern. This up-to-the-
minute wallhanging seems to have it all: rich colors, diminutive houses,
bold strip piecing, and a dazzling set. Hand and machine quilting add
touch-me texture in a comfortable blending of old and new.

BEFORE YOU BEGIN

This quilt is rated challenging primarily because of its unusual setting, which involves set-in seams. In addition, each of the nine blocks has a different arrangement of setting triangles. But don't be intimidated! If you read through the directions and study the diagrams carefully, you'll discover familiar quick-cutting and strip-piecing methods for making the setting triangles and squares. Plus, the small-scale houses use paper foundation piecing, so you can achieve expert accuracy without having to cut tiny pieces from templates.

You will need to make nine copies of the Block Pattern on page 22. Trace the blocks or photocopy them on a high-quality photocopier that won't distort their shape. If you trace the blocks by hand, be sure to copy the numbers, as they indicate the piecing order for the block.

You may also want to refer to "Schoolhouse Basics," beginning on page 104, which contains more detailed instructions to help you with rotary cutting, strip piecing, and set-in seams.

Quilt Size

Finished Quilt Size	29" × 29"
Finished Block Size	
House Block	4"
Overall Block	7"
Number of Blocks	9

NOTE: Due to the number of block variations and the specific block arrangement required for this quilt, no variations in size or layout are provided.

Materials

	Amount
Fuchsia/blue/green plaid	½ yard
Dark blue-violet print	¼ yard
Medium blue-violet print	½ yard
Navy solid	⅔ yard
Tan stripe	⅛ yard
Medium blue-green print	⅛ yard
Purple-and-green plaid	⅛ yard
Teal solid	⅛ yard
Sky blue mottled print	¼ yard
Medium blue streaky print	⅛ yard
Light purple mottled print	⅛ yard
Dark blue swirly print	⅛ yard
Fuchsia solid	⅛ yard
Medium purple solid	⅛ yard
Dark purple solid	⅛ yard
Dark blue-violet solid	⅛ yard
Medium gray solid	⅛ yard
Dusty blue solid	⅛ yard
Light blue solid	⅛ yard
Backing	1 yard
Batting	33" × 33"

NOTE: Yardages are based on 44/45-inch-wide fabrics that are at least 42 inches wide after preshrinking.

Cutting Chart

Fabric	Used For	Strip Width	Number to Cut
Fuchsia/blue/green plaid	Borders	3"	4
Dark blue-violet print	Borders	¾"	4
	Pieced squares and triangles	1"	2
Medium blue-violet solid	Row 1	1½"	2
	Row 2	2½"	1
	Setting triangles	Template A	8
	Setting triangles	Template B	4
Navy solid	Row 1	1½"	2
	Pieced squares and triangles	1"	2
Tan stripe	Row 1	1½"	1
Medium blue-green print	Row 1	1½"	1
Purple-and-green plaid	Row 2	3"	1
Teal solid	Row 3	1¾"	1
Sky blue mottled print	Row 2	2"	2
	Row 3	1¾"	2
Medium blue streaky print	Setting triangles	Template A	8
Light purple mottled print	Setting triangles	Template A	8
Dark blue swirly print	Setting triangles	Template A	4
Fuchsia, medium purple, dark purple, and dark blue-violet solids	Pieced triangles	1⅛"	2 each color
Medium gray, dusty blue, and light blue solids	Pieced triangles and squares	1"	2 each color

CHOOSING FABRICS

This quiltmaker chose her favorite purples, fuchsias, and teals to add richness and depth to her contemporary-looking design. You might enjoy duplicating this cool color palette or prefer an autumn look of reds, golds, browns, and rusts.

To develop your own color scheme for this quilt, photocopy the **Color Plan** on page 23, and experiment with different color arrangements.

CUTTING

All of the measurements include ¼-inch seam allowances. Refer to the Cutting Chart and cut the required strips, cutting across the fabric width.

Make templates for patterns A and B on page 22. See page 116 for details on making and using templates. To trace the templates onto fabric, place them right side up on the wrong side of the fabric.

Note: Cut and piece one sample block before cutting all the fabric for the quilt.

PIECING THE HOUSE BLOCKS

The blocks are pieced in three sections, which are joined to complete the block. Refer to the **Block Diagram** for color placement as you assemble each block. Notice that the strip widths give ample seam allowances. After stitching, simply trim the excess fabric with your scissors or rotary cutter, taking care not to cut through the paper.

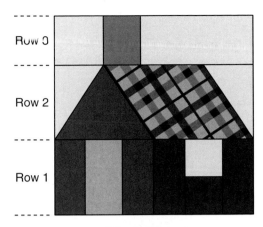

Block Diagram

Step 1. To make Row 1, you will need the following strips: navy, blue-green print, medium blue-violet solid, and tan stripe. To form the window, begin with the navy and blue-green strips and place them right sides together with the navy strip on top. Hold the strips underneath your paper pattern so that they are underneath section 2 (the navy fabric will be against the paper). The edges of the strips should extend at least ¼ inch beyond the boundaries of section 2 on all sides, as shown in **Diagram 1.** Pin in place. Stitch along the line between sections 1 and 2, extending the stitching slightly beyond both ends of the line, as shown.

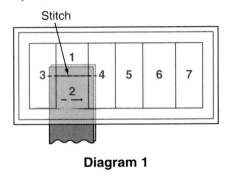

Diagram 1

Step 2. Turn the paper over, trim the seam to ¼ inch, and then open out the strips. Press. Trim the strips so that the navy extends at least ¼ inch beyond the bottom of section 2 and the blue-green extends ¼ inch beyond the top of section 1.

Step 3. With the fabric side of the block facing you, lay the remainder of the navy strip on top of

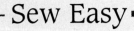

— Sew Easy —

When stitching to paper foundations, set your machine stitch length shorter than usual. Tiny stitches make it easier to tear away the paper, since there are more perforations in the paper. Your stitches will also be more stable as you tug away the paper.

the section 1 and 2 pieces, *with right sides together* and raw edges even on the right edge, as shown in **Diagram 2A.** Holding the strip in place, flip the paper over, and stitch along the line between section 3 and sections 1 and 2. Again, start and stop stitching slightly beyond the ends of the line, as shown in **2B.** Turn the paper over, trim the seam to ¼ inch. Open out the strips and press. Trim the navy strip so that it extends ¼ inch beyond section 3 on all raw edges.

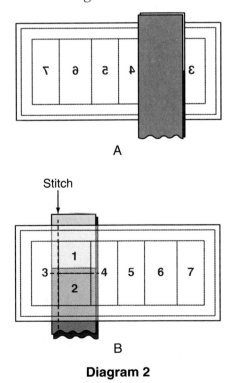

Diagram 2

Step 4. Continue adding fabric, following the numerical order on the pattern. Section 4 will be another navy piece, followed by a blue-violet piece, a tan stripe piece, and a blue-violet piece. Remember to trim the seams each time after you stitch to avoid bulk in the finished block. Also, be sure to leave enough fabric for a seam when you trim beyond the block boundaries.

Step 5. Row 2 is completed in exactly the same fashion as Row 1, except the seam lines are diagonal. Since you'll be sewing to a paper foundation, your fabric will be stabilized and will not stretch as you sew along the bias edge. Begin with the purple-and-green plaid strip for the roof and the sky blue mottled strip for the sky. Hold the strips with right sides together with the plaid strip on top. Then align the strips underneath the paper foundation, as shown in **Diagram 3,** so that you will have enough fabric to cover sections 1 and 2 when the strips are opened up.

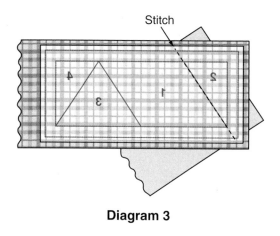

Diagram 3

Step 6. Continue piecing Row 2, adding the medium blue-violet strip for the roof peak (section 3) and finishing with the remainder of the sky blue mottled strip for section 4.

Step 7. Row 3 is pieced from sky blue mottled strips and teal solid strips. Hold the strips with right sides together and the blue strip on top. Place the Row 3 paper foundation over the strips, as shown in **Diagram 4,** so that at least ¼ inch extends beyond the top and bottom of the row for seams. Stitch along the line between sections 1 and 2. Turn the paper over, trim the seam, and open up the strips. Press. Trim excess fabric,

leaving enough to extend beyond the block boundaries for seams. Add the remaining section of Row 3 in the same manner.

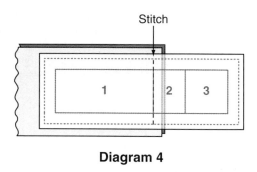

Diagram 4

Step 8. Turn all three rows so the paper side is face up. Using your rotary-cutting equipment, trim the excess fabric and paper from the three sections of the block. Be sure to trim on the dashed outer lines, not the inner solid seam lines. See **Diagram 5.**

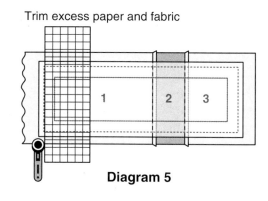

Diagram 5

Step 9. With the paper foundations still in place for stability, sew Row 1 to Row 2. Sew exactly on the dashed seam line. Sew Row 3 to the top of Row 2 in the same manner. When the block is complete, remove the papers, taking care not to stretch the seams. Use tweezers where seams intersect to get out the last bits of paper.

Step 10. Repeat Steps 1 through 9 to complete nine House blocks.

PIECING THE SETTING TRIANGLES AND SQUARES

Some of the setting triangles are strip pieced, while some are cut from a single fabric. For the strip-pieced triangles, sew together strip sets first, then use the triangle template to cut the triangle from the strip set. The same template is used to cut the single-fabric triangles.

Step 1. Sew together 1⅛-inch-wide fuchsia, medium purple, dark purple, and dark blue-violet solid strips along their long edges to form strip sets. Press all seams in one direction. Make a total of 12 strip sets. See **Diagram 6.**

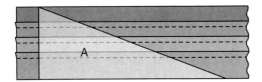

Diagram 6

Step 2. Lay template A *right* side up on the *wrong* side of the strip set, with the long straight edge of the template aligned with the raw edge of the fuchsia strip, as shown. Lay your rotary ruler along one edge of the template to cut one side of the triangle. Repeat along the other triangle side. Cut a total of 12 purple pieced A triangles.

Step 3. The blue pieced A triangles are made in the same manner. Sew together 1-inch-wide dark blue-violet print, navy, medium gray, dusty blue, and light blue strips along their long edges to form strip sets. Press all seams in one direction. See **Diagram 7.** Following the procedure described in Step 2, cut four blue pieced A triangles, with the *longest* edge of template A aligned with the raw edge of the light blue strip, as shown.

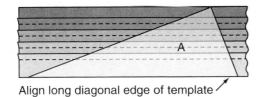

Align long diagonal edge of template

Diagram 7

Step 4. From the leftover blue strip set, cut four 3-inch-wide squares and set them aside.

Devote your valuable time to stitching instead of searching! Keep an extra pack of needles, a spare lightbulb, a few bobbins filled with neutral-color thread, and the instruction manual close at hand when you begin any machine-sewing project.

ASSEMBLING THE BLOCKS

There are nine blocks in this quilt. Each is composed of a House block surrounded by four A triangles. In addition to the purple and blue pieced A triangles, some of the A triangles are cut from a dark blue swirly print, a medium blue streaky print, and a light purple mottled print.

Although the blocks are pieced in exactly the same manner, each has a different color placement and arrangement of the triangles that surround the center block. Refer to the **Assembly Diagram** for color placement and to **Diagram 8** on page 20 for stitching assistance. It is helpful to use a design wall or other flat surface to lay out the blocks before you begin piecing them. For each block variation, posi-

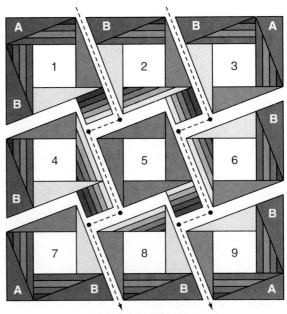

Assembly Diagram

tion the bottom triangle first and work clockwise as you stitch the triangles to the House block.

Step 1. Sew the appropriate A triangle to the bottom edge of the House block, as shown in **Diagram 8A.** With right sides together, align the short edge of the triangle with the left edge of the House block. The long pointy tail of the triangle will extend beyond the right edge of the House block. Stop sewing approximately 1 inch from the raw edge on the right of the House block, as indicated by the arrow. This seam will be finished after the last triangle has been added. Press the seam away from the House block.

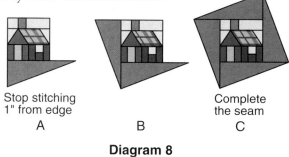

Stop stitching
1" from edge
A

Complete
the seam
C

B

Diagram 8

Step 2. Sew the appropriate A triangle to the left edge of the House block, as shown in **8B.** Align the short edge of the triangle with the top edge of the House block. This time sew the complete seam. Press the seam toward the triangle.

Step 3. Continue adding the remaining triangles to the block, sewing the top triangle next, then the right triangle, in the same manner as in Step 2. When the last triangle has been added, go back and complete the first unfinished seam, sewing in the direction of the arrow in **8C.** Press.

Step 4. Repeat Steps 1 through 3 to complete all nine blocks.

ASSEMBLING THE QUILT TOP

Step 1. Refer to the **Assembly Diagram** on page 19 and use a design wall or other flat surface to lay out the blocks, the strip-pieced squares, and the medium blue-violet A and B setting triangles. The diagram is number coded to indicate which block variation should appear in each position in the quilt top. Refer to the photograph on page 14 for additional assistance.

Step 2. Sew a pieced square to the lower right corner of Block 1, as shown in **Diagram 9.** Press the seam away from the square. Repeat for Blocks 2, 4, and 5.

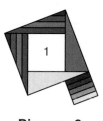

Diagram 9

Step 3. Referring again to the **Assembly Diagram** for positioning, sew the medium blue-violet setting triangles to the outer edges of the house blocks. Note that some blocks have both A and B triangles added, while others have only B triangles. The center block has no setting triangles. Press all seams toward the setting triangles.

Step 4. From this point on, all of the blocks are sewn together with set-in seams. Refer to page 109 for additional information on set-in seams. The blocks are sewn in vertical rows of three blocks each. Then the vertical rows are sewn together.

First, sew Block 1 to Block 4, as illustrated in **Diagram 10.** Begin stitching ¼ inch from the raw edge where the pieced square and Block 1 meet. Sew from the inner corner outward in each direction, as indicated by the arrows. Press the seams as desired. In a similar fashion, sew Block 4 to Block 7 to complete the first row.

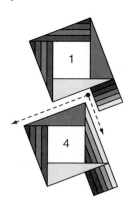

Diagram 10

Quilt Diagram

Step 5. Using the same procedure, complete the second vertical row by sewing Block 2 to Block 5, then Block 5 to Block 8. Complete the third row by sewing together Blocks 3, 6, and 9.

Step 6. Sew the rows together, stitching in the direction indicated by the arrows in the **Assembly Diagram.** Stop stitching and pivot ¼ inch from the raw edges at each corner marked with a dot. Press as desired.

ADDING THE BORDERS

Step 1. Sew the dark blue-violet print border strips to the fuchsia/blue/green plaid border strips in four pairs. Press the seams toward the plaid strips. Trim each to 31 inches long.

Step 2. Fold a border in half crosswise and crease. Unfold it and position it right side down along one side of the quilt top, with the crease at the quilt's horizontal midpoint. The narrow blue-

violet strip should be positioned so that, when sewn, it is closest to the center of the quilt. Pin and sew the border in place, using a ¼-inch seam. Begin and end sewing ¼ inch from the raw edge of the quilt top. Repeat this procedure to attach the remaining borders to the other three sides of the quilt top. Press seams away from the borders.

Step 3. Miter the corner seams, carefully matching the seams of the two border fabrics, as shown in the **Quilt Diagram.** Refer to page 119 for complete details on mitering corners.

QUILTING AND FINISHING

Step 1. Mark the quilt top for quilting. In the quilt shown, the House blocks are hand quilted in the ditch. The triangles around the center house are hand quilted in a swirly motif that follows the pattern of the fabric. The strip-pieced triangles are machine quilted in the ditch, with straight lines echoed in the unpieced triangles. The outer

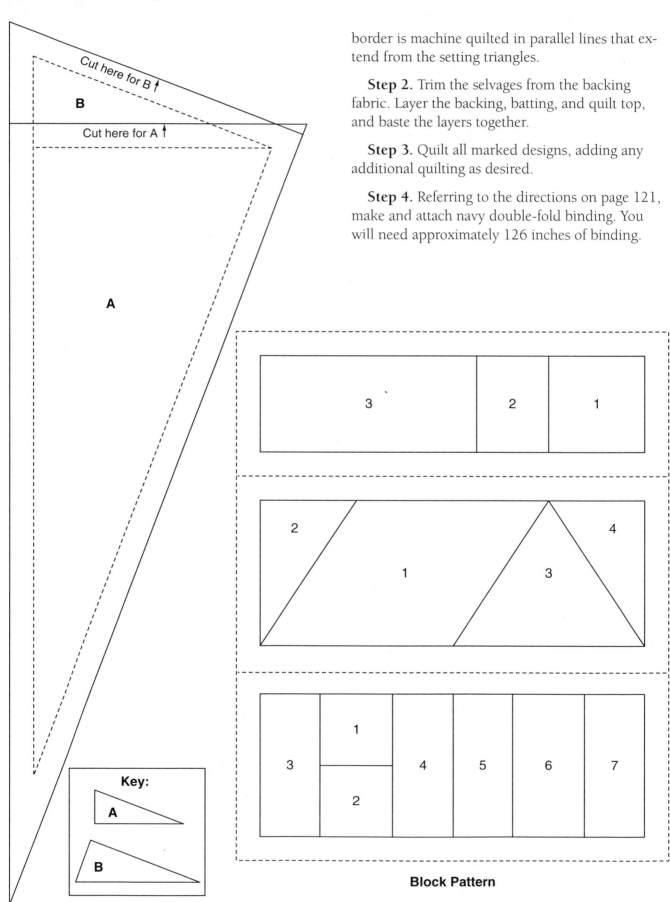

border is machine quilted in parallel lines that extend from the setting triangles.

Step 2. Trim the selvages from the backing fabric. Layer the backing, batting, and quilt top, and baste the layers together.

Step 3. Quilt all marked designs, adding any additional quilting as desired.

Step 4. Referring to the directions on page 121, make and attach navy double-fold binding. You will need approximately 126 inches of binding.

Cut here for B ↑

B

Cut here for A ↑

A

Key:

A

B

Block Pattern

THE ECLECTIC NEIGHBORHOOD

Color Plan

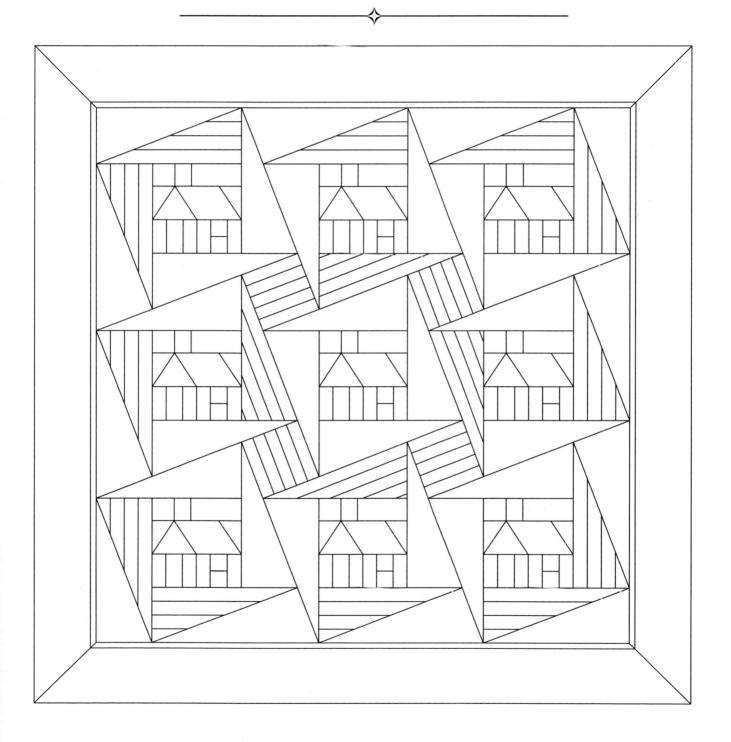

Photocopy this page and use it to experiment with color schemes for your quilt.

HOMESPUN HOUSES

Skill Level: *Easy*

An abundant collection of country plaids, checks, and stripes lends a "welcome home" feeling to Gerry Sweem's rendition of this old-time favorite design. Take the chill off a cold winter evening with this cozy king-size charmer, or scale it down in size for a special child.

———————————◆———————————

BEFORE YOU BEGIN

With the exception of a few simple shapes that require templates, most of the pieces are strips that can be rotary cut. Fabrics can be layered for even more efficient cutting.

You'll find general information and special tips to help you in constructing the basic Schoolhouse block in "Schoolhouse Basics," beginning on page 104.

CHOOSING FABRICS

While the set of this quilt is simple and straightforward, the choice of fabric makes it something truly special. Except for the borders, where specific yardages are required, each block is a scrap-happy combination that utilizes small bits and pieces of various plaid, checked, and striped fabrics in rich country shades.

It may take a little while to collect the variety of fabrics needed, but the end result is definitely worth it. You may want to substitute an occasional floral, paisley, or other print fabric to help you reach your goal.

The **Block Diagram** on page 27 is shaded to indicate placement of the key fabrics. There are two main fabrics in each block:

Quilt Sizes		
	Twin	King (shown)
Finished Quilt Size	65" × 88"	99½" × 99½"
Finished Block Size	11½"	11½"
Number of Blocks	24	49

Materials		
	Twin	King
Dark brown check	2⅛ yards	2½ yards
Tan plaid	2¼ yards	2¾ yards
Black-and-brown plaid	2⅜ yards	2⅞ yards
Assorted plaids, checks, and stripes	3¾ yards	6 yards
Backing	5¼ yards	9 yards
Batting	73" × 96"	108" × 108"
Binding	¾ yard	⅞ yard

NOTE: Yardages are based on 44/45-inch-wide fabrics that are at least 42 inches wide after preshrinking.

the "schoolhouse" fabric and the "background" fabric. The other fabrics can match each other or not, according to your preference. In some blocks, you may select the same fabric for the door, windows, and chimneys. In another block, you may experiment with a different fabric for each. The ultimate decision will be made by the number and size of the fabrics in your collection

and how scrappy a look you'd like in the finished quilt.

You'll notice there is no specific light/dark formula for the blocks in this quilt. Sometimes, the house is dark while the background is light. In other blocks, the opposite is true. The key is to maintain some contrast in value so the house stands out against the sky, and the door and windows are distinguishable from the rest of the

Cutting Chart

Fabric	Used For	*Lengthwise* Strip Width	Number to Cut Twin	King
Dark brown check	Border 1	2"	4	4
Tan plaid	Border 2	3½"	4	4
Black-and-brown plaid	Border 3	5½"	4	4
Red plaid	Binding	27" × 27"	1	
		31" × 31"		1

Fabric	Used For	Dimensions	Number to Cut per Block
Each Schoolhouse plaid	L	1¾" × 6¼"	1
	G	1¾" × 5½"	1
	I	1¾" × 3¾"	1
	M	1½" × 6¼"	1
	K	1½" × 3¾"	2
	C	Template C	1
Each block background	H	1¼" × 6¼"	1
	N	1¼" × 6¼"	1
	B	Template B	1
	O	2½" × 4"	1
	Q	2½" × 3"	2
	D and D reverse	Template D	1 each
Each window plaid	J	1¾" × 3¾"	2
Each door plaid	E	2" × 5½"	1
Each chimney plaid	P	2" × 2½"	2
Each roof plaid	A	Template A	1

house. The contrast can be as strong or as subtle as you wish, but a mix of light and dark houses and high and low contrast blocks makes for the most visually exciting quilt. Don't be afraid to experiment!

CUTTING

All measurements include ¼-inch seam allowances. Referring to the Cutting Chart, cut the required number of strips in the sizes needed. Cut border strips along the *lengthwise* grain (parallel to the selvage). Strips for the Schoolhouse blocks may be cut either lengthwise or crosswise.

For ease of construction, rotary cutting dimensions are given with the **Block Diagram.** For example, the piece labeled G does not require a template to cut. The letter label is given for easy reference. Because some of the pieces are similar but not identical, it is helpful to label your stacks of pieces by their letters.

Make templates for pieces A, B, C, and D using the full-size pattern pieces on page 30. See page 116 for complete details on making and using templates. Cut one piece A, B, C, D, and D reverse for each block, as directed in the Cutting Chart. Place templates A and D wrong side up on the wrong side of the fabric to trace your pieces. Then turn template D over to trace D reverse pieces.

In the quilt shown, the block in the top left corner is facing the opposite direction from all of the other houses. To make a similar block for your quilt, you will need to cut the A and B pieces for that block with the template right side up on the wrong side of the fabric.

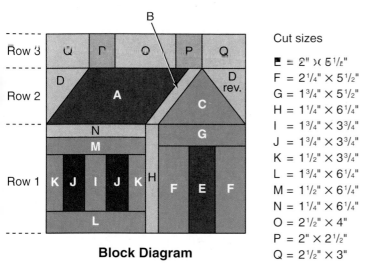

Cut sizes	
E	= 2" × 5½"
F	= 2¼" × 5½"
G	= 1¾" × 5½"
H	= 1¼" × 6¼"
I	= 1¾" × 3¾"
J	= 1¾" × 3¾"
K	= 1½" × 3¾"
L	= 1¾" × 6¼"
M	= 1½" × 6¼"
N	= 1¼" × 6¼"
O	= 2½" × 4"
P	= 2" × 2½"
Q	= 2½" × 3"

Block Diagram

Note: Cut and piece one sample block before cutting all the fabric for the quilt.

PIECING THE SCHOOLHOUSE BLOCKS

Refer to the **Block Diagram** as you assemble each block. Before stitching any units together, lay out all the pieces for one block to ensure that you're happy with your fabric choices.

Step 1. To make the front of the house, sew an F house fabric piece to either side of an E door fabric piece along the long sides, as shown in **Diagram 1**. Press seams toward the darker fabric. Add a G house fabric strip above the door, then sew an H background fabric strip to the left of the unit, referring to the diagram. In each case, press the seam toward the newly added piece.

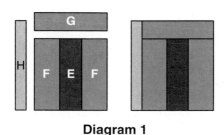

Diagram 1

Step 2. Sew a J window fabric piece to either side of an I house fabric piece along the long sides. Add K house fabric strips to each end of the unit, referring to **Diagram 2**. Press all seams toward the darker fabric. Add an L house fabric piece to the

bottom of the window unit and an M house fabric piece along the top edge. Then sew an N background fabric strip to the top of the window unit, as shown. In each case, press the seam toward the newly added piece.

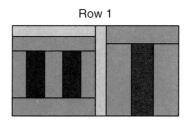

Diagram 2

Step 3. Join the house front to the window unit, as shown in **Diagram 3**, to complete Row 1. Press the seam toward the house front and set aside.

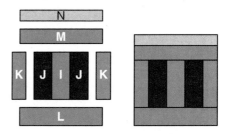

Diagram 3

Step 4. Sew an A, B, C, D, and D reverse piece together to form Row 2, as shown in **Diagram 4**. The C house peak should be cut from your house fabric, and the D and D reverse pieces should match the background fabric in Row 1. Choose any contrasting fabric for the A roof piece. Press the seams so they are in the opposite direction of the seams they will meet in Row 1, then set aside.

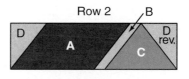

Diagram 4

Step 5. For Row 3, sew a P chimney fabric piece to either side of an O background fabric piece. Sew a Q background fabric piece to each end of the row. See **Diagram 5.** Press the seams to one side.

Row 3

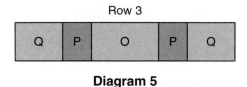

Diagram 5

Step 6. Join Rows 1, 2, and 3, referring to the **Block Diagram** on page 27. Carefully match any appropriate seams. Press the seams as desired.

Step 7. Repeat Steps 1 through 6, making 24 blocks for the twin or 49 blocks for the king.

Step 8. To make an opposite facing block, as in the top left corner of the quilt shown, piece one of your blocks with the house front unit sewn to the left of the window unit. Then piece Row 2 in reverse order, using the A and B pieces cut with the template right side up on the fabric. Row 3 is constructed in the same manner as for all other blocks.

ASSEMBLING THE QUILT TOP

Step 1. Referring to the **Quilt Diagram,** lay out the Schoolhouse blocks for a pleasing visual balance of lights and darks and occasional brights.

Step 2. Sew the blocks together in horizontal rows. Press the seams in opposite directions from row to row. Sew the rows together, carefully matching seams where the blocks meet. Press.

ADDING THE BORDERS

This quilt is surrounded by three borders, and each is added in the same sequence: the two side strips are attached first, followed by the top and bottom strip of the same fabric. Piece together border strips, referring to page 119. Then, following the directions below, trim them to the necessary length when they are added to the quilt top.

The procedure for adding borders is the same whether you are making the twin-size or the king-size quilt. Only the length of the strips will vary.

······· Sew Quick·········

Occasionally woven plaids and stripes lose body when washed, making them limp and troublesome when cutting and stitching. A light touch of spray starch (and a moderately hot, dry iron) will restore crispness.

Step 1. Measure the quilt from top to bottom, taking the measurement through the center of the quilt, not the sides. Cut two dark brown check side borders to this length.

Step 2. Fold one strip in half crosswise and crease. Unfold it and position it right side down along one side of the quilt top, with the crease at the quilt's center. Pin at the center and ends first, then along the entire side, easing in fullness if necessary. Sew the border to the quilt top. Press the seam toward the border. Repeat on the opposite side.

Step 3. Measure the width of the quilt through the horizontal center of the quilt and including the side borders. Cut two dark brown check border strips to this length. In the same manner as for the side borders, position, pin, and stitch the border to the quilt top. Press the seam toward the border. Repeat on the opposite end.

Step 4. In the same manner, add the tan plaid borders to the sides, then the top and bottom of the quilt top, followed by the black-and-brown plaid border strips.

QUILTING AND FINISHING

Step 1. Mark the quilt top for quilting. The quilt shown is quilted in an overall Baptist Fan pattern, as shown in **Diagram 6.**

Diagram 6

Twin   King

Twin

King

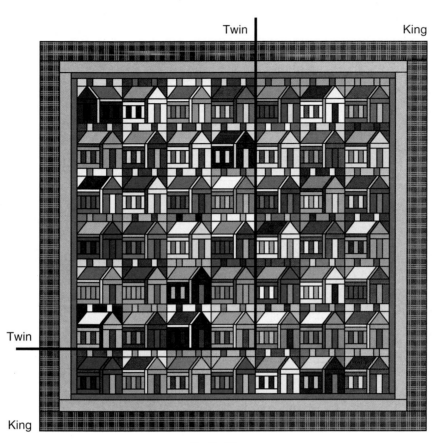

Quilt Diagram

Step 2. Regardless of which size quilt you're making, you'll need to piece the backing. For the twin-size quilt, cut the backing fabric in half crosswise, and trim the selvages. Cut one piece in half lengthwise, and sew one half to each side of the full-width piece. Press seams away from the center.

For the king-size quilt, cut the backing fabric crosswise into three equal pieces. Trim the selvages and sew the pieces together along the long edges. Press the seams away from the center panel. See page 111 for more information on making quilt backings.

Step 3. Layer the backing, batting, and quilt top; baste the layers together.

Step 4. Quilt all marked designs, adding any additional quilting as desired.

Step 5. Referring to the directions on page 121, make and attach double-fold bias binding. Use the square of red plaid fabric that has been set aside for this purpose. For the twin-size quilt, you will need approximately 316 inches; for the king-size quilt, you will need approximately 408 inches.

Sew Easy

The yardage requirements for this quilt include enough fabric to cut the border strips lengthwise from the fabric so you can take advantage of the stability of the lengthwise grain and eliminate the need for seaming.

Use the leftovers creatively—in some of the house blocks, to make a hanging sleeve, or for a quilt label. Or, like the maker of this quilt, plan a special design for a completely reversible quilt!

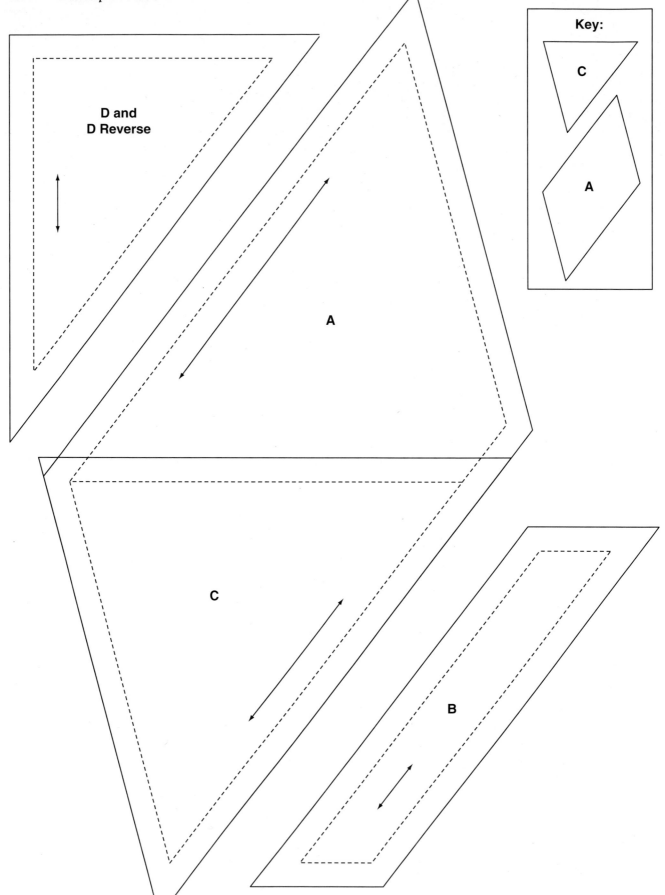

**D and
D Reverse**

A

C

B

Key:

C

A

HOMESPUN HOUSES
Color Plan

Photocopy this page and use it to experiment with color schemes for your quilt.

ALL-AMERICAN SCHOOLHOUSES

Skill Level: *Easy*

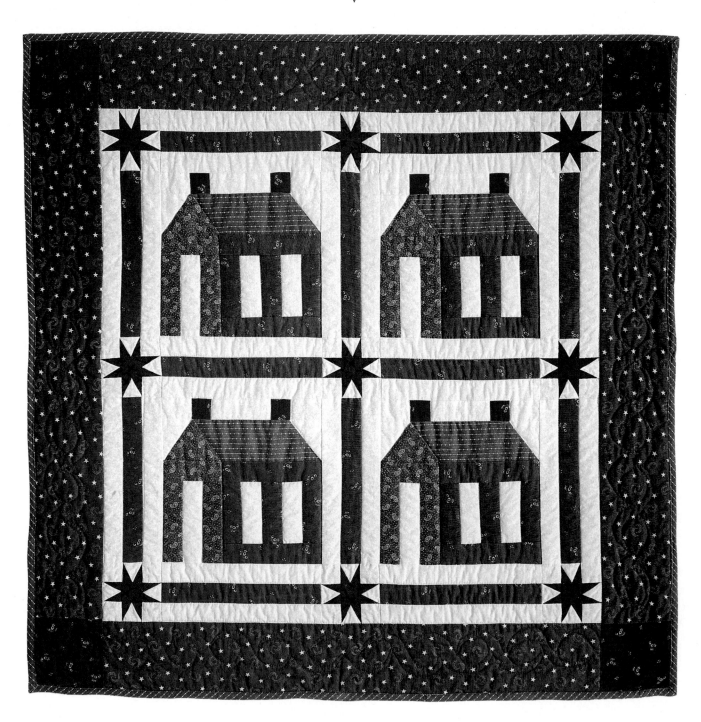

*T*winkling stars and bold striped sashing add patriotic flair to the time-honored Schoolhouse motif in this quilt pieced by Sharyn Craig. With its ample helping of red, white, and blue, this wallhanging is the perfect accent for Independence Day or any day! Most of the strips for this all-American beauty are the same width, so rotary cutting is a breeze.

———————————◆———————————

BEFORE YOU BEGIN

With the exception of a few simple shapes that require templates, all of the pieces are strips and squares that can be rotary cut. In addition, an easy strip-piecing technique is provided for making the pieced sashing and parts of the Schoolhouse block. Strips of fabric are sewn together into sets, which are cut into smaller units that are used as sashing or incorporated into the Schoolhouse blocks.

"Schoolhouse Basics," beginning on page 104, provides general information about making Schoolhouse blocks and details on strip-piecing techniques.

CHOOSING FABRICS

This quiltmaker stretched the traditional red, white, and blue color scheme to encompass burgundy and dusty blue, giving this quilt a popular country look. You might prefer the more traditional bright red and deep navy for your all-American tribute. A subtle white-on-white print adds visual texture.

To develop your own color scheme for the quilt, photocopy the **Color Plan** on page 39, and use crayons or colored pencils to experiment with different color arrangements.

Quilt Sizes

	Wallhanging (shown)	Crib
Finished Quilt Size	33½" × 33½"	44½" × 55½"
Finished Block Size		
Schoolhouse	8"	8"
Star	3"	3"
Number of Blocks		
Schoolhouse	4	12
Star	9	20

Materials

	Wallhanging	Crib
White-on-white print	⅞ yard	1½ yards
Dark blue star print	⅝ yard	⅞ yard
Dark dusty blue print	⅝ yard	1 yard
Medium dusty blue stripe	⅝ yard	⅔ yard
Medium dusty blue print	¼ yard	⅜ yard
Burgundy print	¼ yard	¼ yard
Red-and-black print	¼ yard	⅜ yard
Backing	1⅛ yards	2¾ yards
Batting	38" × 38"	51" × 62"

NOTE: *Yardages are based on 44/45-inch-wide fabrics that are at least 42 inches wide after preshrinking.*

CUTTING

All of the measurements include ¼-inch seam allowances. Referring to the Cutting Chart,

33

Cutting Chart

Fabric	Used For	Strip Width or Piece	Number to Cut Wallhanging	Crib	Second Cut Dimensions	Number to Cut Wallhanging	Crib
White-on-white print	Sashing	1½"	6	16			
	Unit 2	1½"	1	2			
	Unit 3	1½"	2	2			
	Unit 1	2"	2	2			
	Unit 1	3½"	1	1			
	C	Template C	4	12			
	C reverse	Template C	4	12			
	G	Template G	36	80			
	I	1½"	2	3	1½" square	36	80
Dark blue star print	Border	4½"	4	5			
Dark dusty blue print	Sashing	1½"	3	8			
	Unit 3	1½"	3	3			
	E	1½"	2	4	1½" × 5½"	8	24
	A	Template A	4	12			
Medium dusty blue stripe	B	Template B	4	12			
Medium dusty blue print	Unit 2	1½"	2	4			
	D	1½"	2	3	1½" × 3½"	4	12
Burgundy print	Unit 1	1½"	2	2			
	Border corners	4¼"	1	1	4¼" squares	4	4
Red-and-black print	F	Template F	36	80			
	F reverse	Template F	36	80			
	H	1½"	1	1	1½" squares	9	20

cut the required number of strips in the widths needed. Cut all strips across the fabric width. Some of the strips will be subcut into shorter lengths, as listed under "Second Cut Dimensions."

Make templates for pieces A, B, and C for the Schoolhouse blocks and F and G for the Star blocks using the full-size patterns on page 38. See page 116 for complete details on making and using templates. The Cutting Chart indicates how many pieces to cut with each template. Place the B, C, and F templates wrong side up on the wrong side of the fabric to trace and cut pieces. For the reverse pieces, turn the C and F templates right side up to cut C reverse and F reverse.

Note: Cut and piece one sample block before cutting all the fabric for the quilt.

PIECING THE SCHOOLHOUSE BLOCKS

Refer to the **Block Diagram** as you assemble each block. For ease of construction, strip-pieced units are numbered as Unit 1, Unit 2, and Unit 3. All other pieces have letter labels. Refer to the Quilt Sizes chart on page 33 to determine how many blocks you will need for your quilt size.

Step 1. Row 3, the sky and chimneys, is made entirely from a Unit 1 strip set. Sew 1½-inch-wide burgundy print strips to either side of a 3-inch-wide white strip. Then sew a 2-inch white strip to each burgundy strip. See **Diagram 1**. Press the seams toward the burgundy strips.

Step 2. Square up one end of the strip set and cut 1½-inch-wide segments from it, as shown,

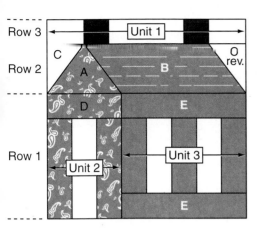

Row 3 ← Unit 1 →

C   O rev.

Row 2   A   B

Row 1

D   E

Unit 2   Unit 3

E

Schoolhouse Block Diagram

Cut sizes

D = 1½" × 3½"
E = 1½" × 5½"

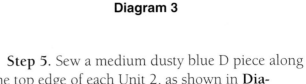

4½"

Diagram 3

until you have one Row 3 for each Schoolhouse block.

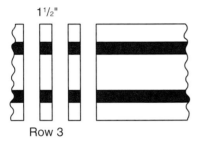

1½"

Row 3

Diagram 1

Step 3. To make Row 2, sew an A, B, C, and C reverse piece together in the sequence shown in **Diagram 2**. Press all seams toward B. Repeat, making a Row 2 for each Schoolhouse block.

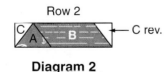

Row 2

C A B ← C rev.

Diagram 2

Step 4. Row 1 is made from Unit 2 and Unit 3 strips sets as well as from the D and E segments. To make the Unit 2 strip set, sew a 1½-inch-wide medium dusty blue print strip to either side of a 1½-inch-wide white strip, as shown in **Diagram 3**. Press the seams toward the blue strips. Square up one end of the strip set, and cut one 4½-inch Unit 2 segment for each Schoolhouse block.

Step 5. Sew a medium dusty blue D piece along the top edge of each Unit 2, as shown in **Diagram 4**. Press the seams toward D.

D

Diagram 4

Step 6. To make a Unit 3 strip set, sew together three 1½-inch-wide dark dusty blue print strips and two 1½-inch-wide white strips, alternating colors, as shown in **Diagram 5**. Press seams toward the blue strips. Square up one end of the strip set, and cut a 3½-inch-wide Unit 3 segment for each Schoolhouse block, as shown.

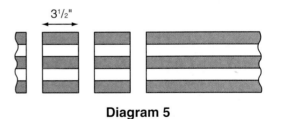

3½"

Diagram 5

Step 7. Sew a dark dusty blue E piece along the top and bottom edges of each Unit 3, as shown in **Diagram 6A**. Press the seams toward E. Sew each of these units to a Unit 2, as shown in **6B**, to complete Row 1. Press the seams toward Unit 2.

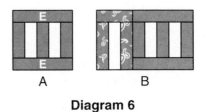

E

E

A   B

Diagram 6

Step 8. Join Rows 1, 2, and 3 of each School-house block, as shown in the **Block Diagram** on page 35. Press the seams as desired.

Sew Easy

An empty fabric bolt makes a great portable ironing board. Wrap it in a thick towel, pin securely, and position it at your sewing station so you can press as you go. You'll save precious time—and you'll be recycling, too!

MAKING THE SASHING STRIPS

Step 1. Sew a 1½-inch-wide white strip to each side of a 1½-inch-wide dark dusty blue strip. See **Diagram 7**. Press the seams toward the blue strip.

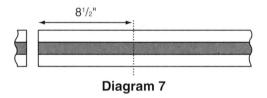

8½"

Diagram 7

Step 2. Square up one end of a set, and cut as many 8½-inch segments as possible from the long strip set. Continue making strip sets and cutting segments until you have assembled 12 sashing strips for the wallhanging or 31 for the crib quilt.

PIECING THE STAR BLOCKS

Step 1. Sew red F and F reverse triangles to either side of a G triangle, as shown in **Diagram 8**. Press the seams toward the red triangles. Make four of these units for each block.

Step 2. Lay out the pieced triangle units and the H and I squares in three rows of three, forming a star, as shown in the **Star Block Diagram**. Sew the squares together into horizontal rows, pressing the seams in opposite directions from row to row. Sew the rows together. Press.

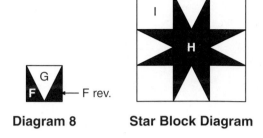

Diagram 8   **Star Block Diagram**

ASSEMBLING THE QUILT TOP

Step 1. Referring to the **Assembly Diagram**, use a design wall or other flat surface to lay out the Schoolhouse blocks, Star blocks, and sashing strips. The quilt in the photograph is a wall-hanging with two rows of two Schoolhouse blocks each. The layout for the crib quilt is the same except it contains four horizontal rows of three Schoolhosue blocks each. In each quilt, the blocks are separated by sashing strips and Star blocks.

Step 2. Sew the Star blocks and sashing strips together into rows, then sew the Schoolhouse blocks and sashing strips into horizontal rows, as

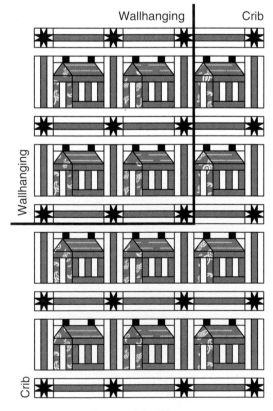

Assembly Diagram

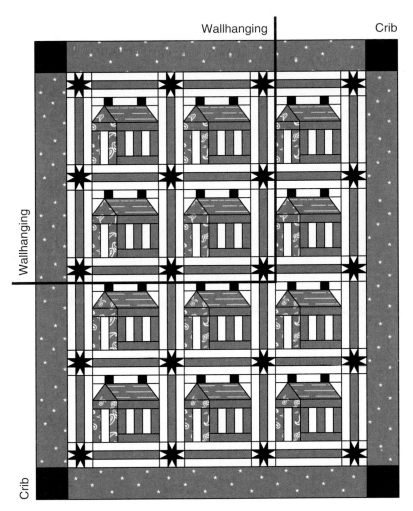

Quilt Diagram

shown in the diagram. Press the seams in opposite directions from row to row. Sew the rows together, carefully matching seams. Press.

ADDING THE BORDERS

Step 1. If you are making the crib quilt, you'll need to piece two long border strips for the side borders. Cut one of the 4½-inch dark blue star print border strips in half, and sew one half each to two of the remaining border strips. See page 119 for details on the diagonal seaming method of connecting border strips. Press the seams open.

Step 2. For either size quilt, measure the length of the quilt, taking the measurement through the vertical center of the quilt, not the sides. Trim two

borders to this length for the *side* borders. Measure the width of the quilt, taking the measurement through the horizontal center of the quilt. Trim the remaining two border strips to this length for the top and bottom borders.

Step 3. Fold one side border strip in half crosswise and crease. Unfold it and position it right side down along one side of the quilt top, with the crease at the horizontal midpoint. Pin at the midpoint and ends first, then along the length of the entire side, easing in fullness if necessary. Sew the border to the quilt top, using a ¼-inch seam allowance. Press the seams toward the border. Repeat on the opposite side.

Step 4. Sew a 4¼-inch burgundy corner square to each end of the top and the bottom border strips, as shown in **Diagram 9.** Press the seams away from the corner squares.

Diagram 9

Step 5. In the same manner as for the side borders, pin a border strip to one end of the quilt, matching seams and easing in fullness. Stitch, using a ¼-inch seam allowance. Press the seams toward the border. Repeat on the opposite end. See the **Quilt Diagram** on page 37.

QUILTING AND FINISHING

Step 1. Mark the quilt top for quilting. The quilt shown is quilted in the ditch around each schoolhouse, star, and sashing strip. The border is quilted in a continuous cable motif.

Step 2. For the crib quilt, you will need to piece the backing. Cut the backing fabric in half crosswise, and trim the selvages. Join the two pieces along the long edges and press the seam open. The seam will run parallel to the top and bottom of the quilt. Refer to page 111 for more information on pieced backings. For the wallhanging, simply trim the backing selvages.

Step 3. Layer the backing, batting, and quilt top; baste. Quilt as desired.

Step 4. Use the dusty blue striped fabric to make and attach double-fold bias binding, referring to page 121. For the wallhanging, you will need 140 inches of binding; for the crib quilt, you will need 206 inches of binding.

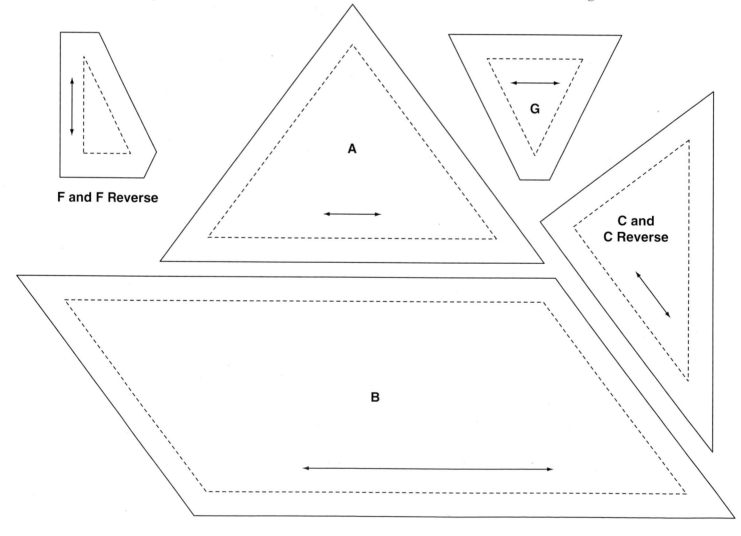

ALL-AMERICAN
SCHOOLHOUSES

Color Plan

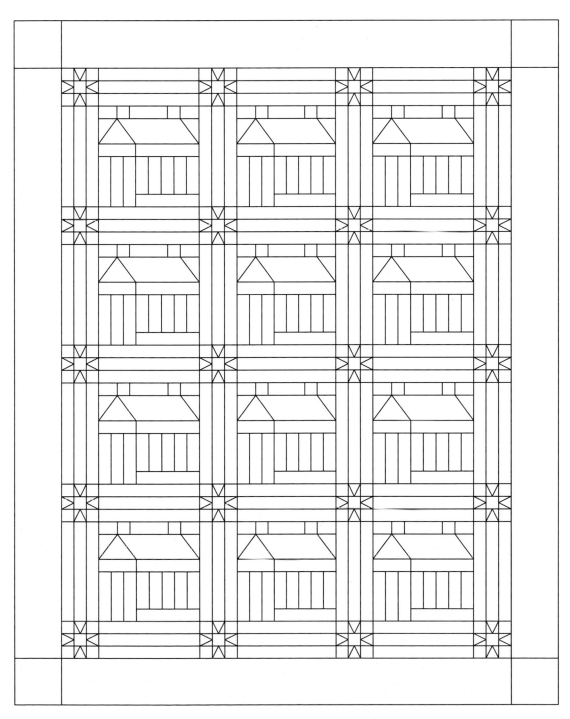

Photocopy this page and use it to experiment with color schemes for your quilt.

LITTLE RED SCHOOLHOUSES

Skill Level: *Easy*

The endearing image of the country schoolhouse springs to life in Mary Stori's nostalgic interpretation of a bona fide classic. The crisp color scheme rings so true, you can almost hear the recess bell! You'll whip up this lap quilt in no time with super-easy strip piecing.

BEFORE YOU BEGIN

With the exception of a few simple shapes that require templates, pieces for this quilt can be rotary cut. An easy strip-piecing technique is used to make the Nine Patch blocks, the pieced sashing, and parts of the Schoolhouse block. "Schoolhouse Basics," beginning on page 104, offers more tips and tricks for piecing your quilt.

CHOOSING FABRICS

The red-and-white scheme enhances this quilt's strong visual appeal, but a similar graphic impact can be created with any high-contrast two-color scheme. Replace the red with navy or spruce for a totally different look. Or substitute a variety of prints in a single color family for more visual texture.

To develop your own color scheme, photocopy the **Color Plan** on page 47, and use colored pencils to experiment with different color arrangements.

CUTTING

All of the measurements include ¼-inch seam allowances. Refer to the Cutting Chart on page 42 and cut the required number of strips in the sizes needed. Cut border strips first, cutting them on the lengthwise grain (parallel to the selvage). The balance of the strips may be cut on the crosswise grain of the fabric.

Referring to the directions on page 116, make templates for pieces A, B, C, and D, using the full-size pattern pieces on page 46. The Cutting Chart lists how many of each piece to cut with each template. Place the templates wrong side up on the wrong side of the fabric to cut the pieces. Turn the D template over to cut the D reverse pieces.

Quilt Sizes

	Lap (shown)	Queen
Finished Quilt Size	56½" × 71¼"	86" × 100¾"
Finished Block Size		
Schoolhouse	11"	11"
Nine Patch	3¾"	3¾"
Number of Blocks		
Schoolhouse	12	30
Nine Patch	20	42

Materials

	Lap	Queen
Red solid	2½ yards	4 yards
Muslin	2⅜ yards	4⅞ yards
Assorted red plaids	½ yard	1 yard
Backing	3½ yards	7⅞ yards
Batting	63" × 78"	92" × 107"
Binding	¾ yard	⅞ yard

NOTE: Yardages are based on 44/45-inch-wide fabrics that are at least 42 inches wide after preshrinking.

Cutting Chart

Fabric	Used For	Strip Width	Number to Cut Lap	Number to Cut Queen
Red solid	Borders	4½"	4	4
	Sashing	1¾"	15	28
	Strip Set 1	2"	2	4
	Strip Set 2	1½"	2	4
	Strip Set 2	1¾"	2	4
	Strip Set 3	1¼"	1	2
	Strip Set 3	1¾"	2	4
	E	1¾"	2	4
	G	1¾"	4	10
	A	Template A	12	30
Muslin	Sashing	1¾"	26	52
	Strip Set 1	2½"	2	4
	Strip Set 1	4½"	1	2
	Strip Set 2	2¼"	2	4
	Strip Set 3	1¾"	2	4
	F	1¾"	2	5
	G	1¾"	2	5
	B	Template B	12	30
	D	Template D	12	30
	D reverse	Template D	12	30
Red plaids	C	Template C	12	30

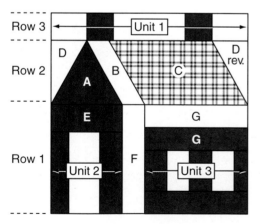

Block Diagram

Cut sizes

E = 1¾" × 4½"
F = 1¾" × 6½"
G = 1¾" × 6¼"

You will need to cut some of the strips into shorter lengths before assembling the Schoolhouse blocks, as follows:

• From the 1¾-inch red E strips, cut one 4½-inch-long E segment for each Schoolhouse block.

• From the 1¾-inch muslin F strips, cut one 6½-inch-long F segment for each Schoolhouse block.

• From the 1¾-inch red and muslin G strips, cut 6¼-inch-long G segments. You'll need two red and one muslin G piece for each Schoolhouse block.

Note: Cut and piece one sample block before cutting all the fabric for the quilt.

PIECING THE SCHOOLHOUSE BLOCKS

Refer to the **Block Diagram** as you assemble the blocks. Rows 1 and 3 are pieced from rotary-cut strips and segments, which are labeled with letters and unit labels for easy reference. Row 2 pieces are cut from templates. Refer to the Quilt Sizes chart on page 41 to determine how many blocks you will need for the size quilt you are making.

Step 1. To make Row 3, sew a 2-inch red strip to either side of a 4½-inch muslin strip. Then add a 2½-inch muslin strip to either side of the red strips to complete Strip Set 1. See **Diagram 1**. Press the seams toward the red strips. Square up one end of the strip set and cut 2-inch segments from it, as shown. For the lap quilt, cut 12 segments. For the queen-size quilt, make two strip sets and cut a total of 30 segments.

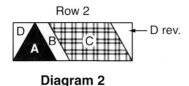

Row 3

Strip Set 1

Diagram 1

Step 2. Sew a red A, a muslin B, a red plaid C, and muslin D and D reverse pieces together, as shown in **Diagram 2**, to complete Row 2 of the Schoolhouse block. Press the seams as desired and set aside. Make one Row 2 for each house.

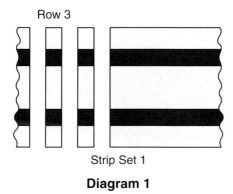

Row 2

D   D rev.
B   C
A

Diagram 2

Step 3. The house fronts are cut from Strip Set 2. To make the strip set, sew a 1½-inch red strip, a 2¼-inch muslin strip, and a 1¾-inch red strip together; see **Diagram 3**. Press seams toward the red strips. Square up one end of the strip set and cut 5-inch segments from it, as shown. Continue to make strip sets and cut segments until you have one unit for each house.

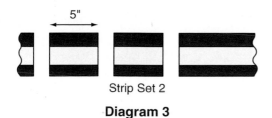

5"

Strip Set 2

Diagram 3

Step 4. Referring to **Diagram 4**, sew a red E rectangle to the top edge of each unit. Add a muslin F segment to the right edge of each unit. Press the seams toward the red fabric.

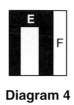

E
F

Diagram 4

Step 5. To make the house sides, first make Strip Set 3. Sew together two red and two muslin 1¾-inch strips, alternating colors. To complete the strip set, add a 1¼-inch red strip to the outer muslin strip. See **Diagram 5**. Press the seams toward the red strips. Square up one end of the strip set and cut 2¾-inch segments from it, as shown. Continue making strip sets and cutting them into segments until you have one segment for each Schoolhouse block.

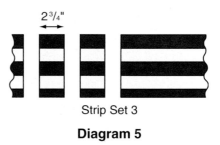

2¾"

Strip Set 3

Diagram 5

Step 6. Referring to **Diagram 6**, sew a red G strip along the top and bottom edges of each segment. Add a muslin G strip along the top edge of each unit, as shown. Press the seams toward the red strip.

Step 7. Join the house fronts and sides in pairs, as shown in **Diagram 7**, to complete Row 1. Press the seams toward the house side.

G
G

G

Diagram 6

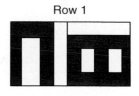

Row 1

Diagram 7

Step 8. Join Rows 1, 2, and 3 of each School-house block, as shown in the **Block Diagram** on page 43, carefully matching appropriate seams. Press the seams as desired.

MAKING THE SASHING

Sashing Strips

Step 1. Sew a 1¾-inch muslin strip to each side of a 1¾-inch red strip, as shown in **Diagram 8**, to form Strip Set A. Press seams toward the red strip.

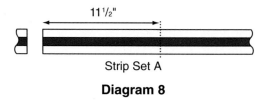

11½"

Strip Set A

Diagram 8

Step 2. Square up one end of the strip set, then cut as many 11½-inch segments from it as possible. Save the leftover strip set pieces for the Nine Patch sashing blocks. Continue making strip sets and cutting segments until you have 31 sashing strips for the lap quilt or 71 for the queen size.

Nine Patch Blocks

Step 1. From the leftover ends of the sashing strips, cut one 1¾-inch A segment for each Nine Patch sashing square.

Step 2. Sew a 1¾-inch red strip to each side of a 1¾-inch muslin strip to make Strip Set B, as shown in **Diagram 9**. Press the seams toward the red strips. Square up one end of the strip set and cut as many 1¾-inch segments as possible. You will need two segments for each Nine Patch sashing block.

Step 3. Sew a B segment to the top and bottom of an A segment, as shown in **Diagram 10**. Press as desired. Repeat to make 20 Nine Patch blocks for the lap quilt or 42 for the queen-size quilt.

Strip Set B

Diagram 9   **Diagram 10**

ASSEMBLING THE QUILT TOP

Step 1. Lay out the Schoolhouse blocks, the Nine Patch blocks, and the sashing strips, referring to the **Partial Lap Assembly Diagram** for placement. The queen-size quilt is laid out in the same manner; however, you will have seven sashing rows and six block rows. The queen-size quilt is five blocks wide.

Partial Lap Assembly Diagram

Step 2. Sew the Nine Patch blocks and horizontal sashing strips together into rows. Sew the Schoolhouse blocks and the vertical sashing strips together into rows. In both types of rows, press the seams toward the sashing strips. Sew the rows together. Press.

ADDING THE BORDERS

Step 1. For either size quilt, measure the quilt top vertically, taking the measurement through the center of the quilt rather than along the sides. Trim two red borders to this length.

Step 2. Fold one strip in half crosswise and crease. Unfold it and position it along one side of the quilt top, with right sides together and the crease at the quilt's horizontal midpoint. Pin at the midpoint and ends first, then along the length of the entire side, easing in fullness if necessary. Sew the border to the quilt top, using a ¼-inch seam. Press the seam toward the border. Repeat, sewing the other border to the opposite side.

Lap | Queen

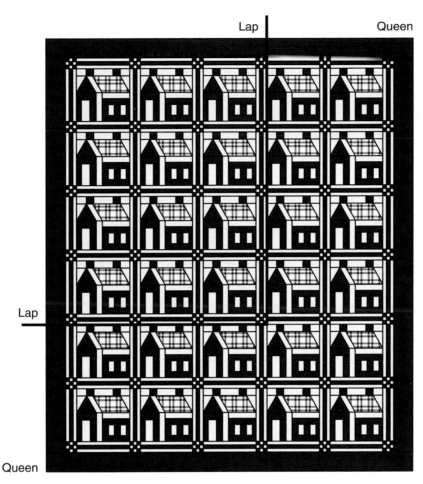

Lap

Queen

Quilt Diagram

Step 3. Measure the width of the quilt through the horizontal center, including the side borders. Trim the remaining red border strips to this length. In the same manner as for the side borders, pin the strips along one end of the quilt top, easing in fullness if necessary. Stitch the borders to the quilt top and press the seams toward the borders. See the **Quilt Diagram.**

QUILTING AND FINISHING

Step 1. Mark the quilt top for quilting. The quilt shown is quilted in pairs of diagonal lines stitched $\frac{1}{4}$ inch apart. The pairs are spaced at 2-inch intervals across the inner portion of the quilt top. The red border is quilted in a series of math equations, such as $2 + 2 = 4$. A miniature Schoolhouse is quilted in each corner.

Step 2. Regardless of which size quilt you're making, the backing will have to be pieced. For the lap quilt, cut the backing fabric in half crosswise and trim the selvages. Join the two pieces along the long edges and press the seam open. For the queen-size quilt, cut the backing fabric crosswise into three equal pieces, and trim the selvages. Sew the pieces together along the long edges, and press the seams away from the center panel. For more information on pieced quilt backs, see page 111.

Step 3. Layer the backing, batting, and quilt top; baste. Quilt as desired.

Step 4. Referring to the directions on page 121, make and attach double-fold bias binding using the red plaid fabric. You will need approximately 264 inches for the lap quilt and 380 inches for the queen size.

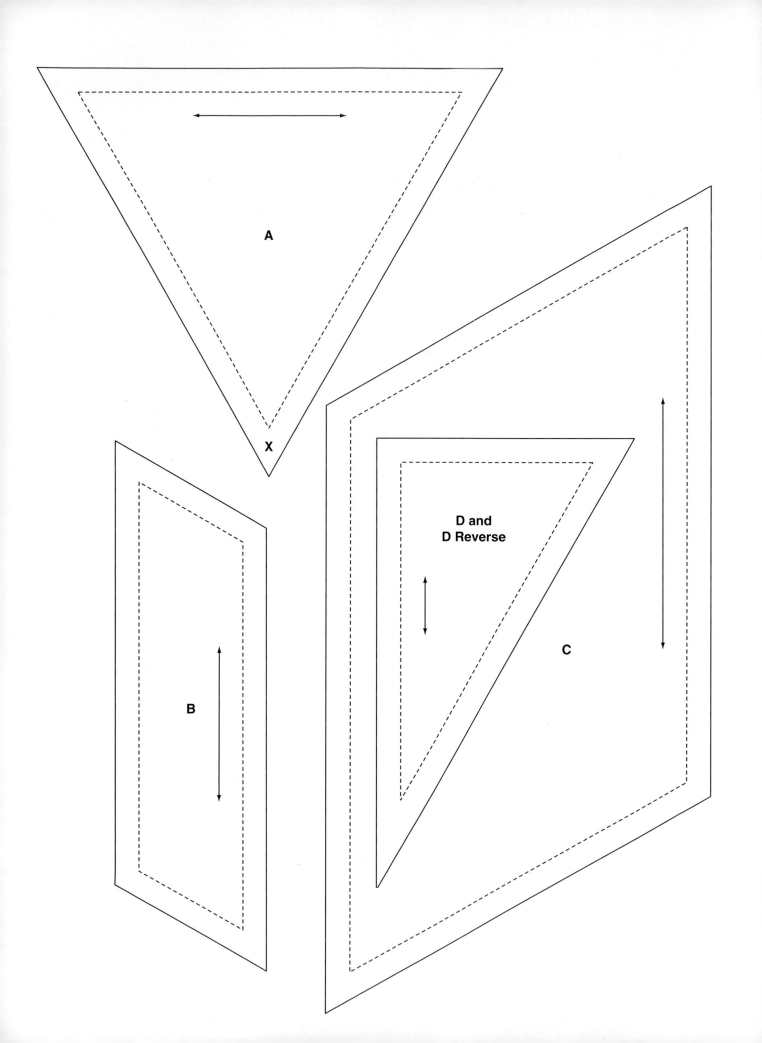

LITTLE RED SCHOOLHOUSES
Color Plan

Photocopy this page and use it to experiment with color schemes for your quilt.

ROW HOUSES

Skill Level: *Challenging*

*J*udy Spahn has combined cool, shimmering colors and an out-of-the-ordinary setting to create a stunning wallhanging or lap quilt with a contemporary twist. The quilt seems to be in motion, and this whirling effect is intensified by the strong diagonal lines of Judy's original border treatment.

Before You Begin

If you study the photograph carefully, you'll notice that this quilt is made of two different House blocks. The blocks are identical, except that House 2 is the reverse of House 1. It is this mirror image, along with the unique arrangement of all 24 House blocks, that gives this quilt its vitality and character.

The instructions are written based on quick-cutting techniques. With the exception of a few simple shapes that require templates, all of the pieces are strips and squares that can be rotary cut. In addition, an easy strip-piecing technique is provided for parts of the House blocks and pieced borders. Strips of fabric are sewn together to form strip sets. These strip sets are then cut apart into individual units that are incorporated into the blocks and borders.

While most of the seams for this quilt require simple, straight-line sewing, a few set-in seams are required. Read through "Set-In Seams" on page 109 to familiarize yourself with the simple procedure for set-in pieces, as well as for more detailed instruc-

tion on the strip-piecing method described above.

Choosing Fabrics

This quiltmaker relied on a variety of solid fabrics in a cool

color scheme of dusty blues, green, teals, lavenders, and grays to give her quilt its sleek, contemporary look. Most of the fabrics are matte finished, but a few are polished cottons, and one or two are not cotton at all but silk shan-

Quilt Size	
Finished Quilt Size	44" × 54½"
Finished Block Size	8"
Number of Blocks	
House 1	20
House 2	4

NOTE: Because the specific block arrangement (including mirror images) is critical to the overall design of the quilt, no variations in size or layout are provided.

Materials	
	Amount
Muslin	1⅓ yards
Assorted dusty blue, green, teal, lavender, and gray solids	2 yards
Navy solid	1¾ yards
Backing	3 yards
Batting	50" × 61"

NOTE: Yardages are based on 44/45-inch-wide fabrics that are at least 42 inches wide after preshrinking.

Cutting Chart

Fabric	Used For	Strip Width or Piece	Number to Cut	Second Cut Dimensions	Number to Cut
Muslin	Unit 1	4"	2		
	Unit 2	4"	1		
	Unit 2	3"	1		
	I	Template I	24		
	I reverse	Template I	24		
	J	1¾"	1	1¾" × 2¾"	4
	Unit 3	2½"	5		
Assorted dusty solids	Unit 3	3"	5		
Navy solid	Border	1"	5		
	Unit 1	1½"	4		
	Unit 2	1½"	2		
	B	1"	3	1" × 4½"	24
	C	1"	4	1" × 6"	24
	D	Template D	20		
	D reverse	Template D	4		
	F	1"	2	1" × 3"	24
	Unit 3	1¼"	10		

From the assorted dusty solids, cut the following pieces for each block. All of the pieces for a single block should be cut from the same fabric. Refer to the *Block Diagram* as needed.

Fabric	Used For	Dimensions	Number to Cut per House
Assorted dusty solids	A	4½" × 5½"	1
	E	Template E*	1
	G	3" × 3"	1
	H	Template H	1

*Cut one E for 20 of the houses and one E reverse for 4 of the houses.

tung. These latter fabrics add sheen and texture that contribute to the quilt's glossy good looks.

For another contemporary look, try working in solids of black, white, and gray. In fact, any mix of neutrals—including beige, brown, taupe, tan, and cream—would make a striking quilt. Or replace the navy framework with black and the muted, dusty tints with rich purples, teals, greens, blues, and pinks for a quilt with a strong Amish flavor.

To help develop a unique color scheme for the quilt, photocopy the **Color Plan** on page 57, and use crayons or colored pencils to experiment with different color arrangements.

CUTTING

All of the measurements include ¼-inch seam allowances. Refer to the Cutting Chart and cut the required number of strips in the sizes needed. Cut all strips across the fabric width (crosswise grain).

Make templates for pieces D, E, H, and I using the full-size pattern pieces on page 56. Refer to page 116 for complete details on making and using templates. The Cutting Chart indicates how many of each piece to cut with each template.

Refer to the **Block Diagram** as you work. For House 1, place the D, E, and I templates wrong

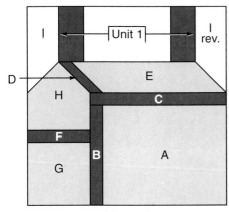

House 1

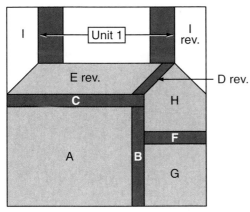

House 2

Block Diagram

Cut sizes

A = 1" × 4½"
B = 5½" × 4½"
C = 6" × 1"
F = 3" × 1"
G = 3" × 3"

side up on the wrong side of the fabric to cut those pieces. Turn the I template over to cut the I reverse pieces.

For House 2, place the D, E, and I templates right side up on the wrong side of the fabric to cut

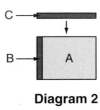

— **Sew Easy**

To prevent fabrics from turning shiny when the seam lines are pressed, press blocks from the reverse side or use a pressing cloth. Always test press a scrap when using unusual fabrics such as silk, wool, or polished cotton to determine the correct temperature setting for your iron.

the D reverse, E reverse, and I reverse pieces. Turn the I template over to cut the I pieces.

Note: Cut and piece one sample block before cutting all the fabric for the quilt.

PIECING THE HOUSE BLOCKS

Refer to the **Block Diagram** as you assemble each block. For ease of construction, each pattern piece is identified by a letter. The strip-pieced chimney unit is labeled Unit 1. In each House block, the A, E, G, and H pieces should be cut from the same fabric. Note that in the House 2 blocks, the D and E pieces are replaced with D reverse and E reverse. You'll need a total of 20 House 1 blocks and four House 2 blocks for this quilt.

House 1 Blocks

Step 1. Pin, then sew a 1½-inch navy strip to either side of a 4-inch muslin strip, as shown in **Diagram 1**. Make another strip set in the same manner, a press all seams toward the navy strips. Using a rotary cutter and ruler, square up one end of each strip set. Cut twenty-four 2¾-inch segments from the strip sets, as shown. Label these segments Unit 1.

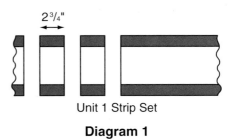

Unit 1 Strip Set

Diagram 1

Step 2. Sew a navy B strip to the right edge of a dusty solid A rectangle, as shown in **Diagram 2**. Press the seams toward B. Add a C segment along the top edge of the A/B unit, as shown, pressing the seams toward C. Set the unit aside.

Diagram 2

Step 3. Sew a D piece to the left edge of E, as shown in **Diagram 3**, to form the roof unit. Press the seams toward E. Join the roof unit to the top of the house, as shown. Press the seams toward C and set aside.

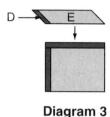

Diagram 3

Step 4. To make the house front, stitch an F strip along one edge of a G square, as shown in **Diagram 4**. Press the seam toward G. Add an H piece to the opposite side of F, pressing the seam toward H.

Diagram 4

Step 5. Sew the house front to the left of the house/roof unit, as shown in **Diagram 5**. Start stitching ¼ inch from the raw edge at the point where the H, D, and C pieces come together, and stitch from this pivot point first in one direction, then in the other, as indicated by the arrows. Refer to page 109 for additional information on pivoted, or set-in, seams.

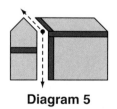

Diagram 5

Step 6. With right sides together, pin, then sew a Unit 1 to the top edge of the house, as shown in **Diagram 6A**.

Begin and end stitching ¼ inch from the raw edges, as shown in **6B**, and press the seams toward the house.

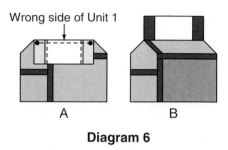

Diagram 6

Step 7. Set in the I and I reverse pieces, as shown in **Diagram 7**. For both of the pieces, begin stitching ¼ inch from the raw edge at the angle where the chimney meets the roof, and stitch to the other edge, as indicated by the arrows in the diagram. Press the seams away from the I pieces.

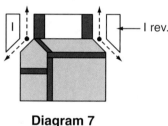

Diagram 7

Step 8. Repeat Steps 1 through 7 to make 20 House 1 blocks.

House 2 Blocks

The House 2 block is assembled in the same fashion as the House 1 block with the following exceptions:

• The A pieces are sewn to the *left* side of the B pieces, as shown in **Diagram 8A**.

• The D reverse pieces are sewn to the *right* edge of the E reverse pieces, as shown in **8B**.

• The house front (G/F/H unit) is stitched to the *right* edge of the house/roof unit.

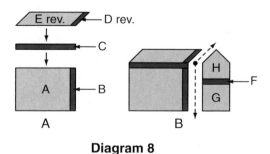

Diagram 8

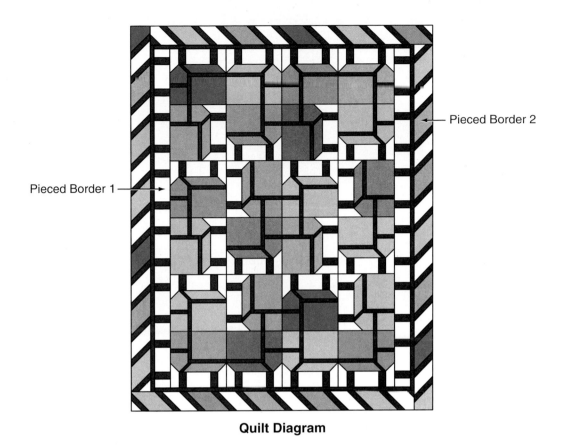

Pieced Border 2

Pieced Border 1

Quilt Diagram

ASSEMBLING THE QUILT TOP

Step 1. Use a design wall or other flat surface to lay out the House blocks exactly as shown in the **Assembly Diagram**. The diagram indicates where

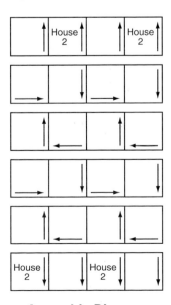

Assembly Diagram

to place the House 2 blocks. Unlabeled squares in the diagram indicate placement of House 1 blocks. For both types of blocks, the arrows show which direction the chimneys of each should be pointing. You may also find it helpful to refer to the photograph on page 48.

Step 2. Sew the blocks together in six horizontal rows, as shown. Each row has four blocks. Press the seams in opposite directions from row to row.

Step 3. Sew the rows together, carefully matching seams where the blocks meet. Press the quilt top.

PIECING THE BORDERS

There are two separate pieced border units for this quilt. Pieced Border 1 (the inner border) is used only on the quilt sides. Pieced Border 2 (the outer, diagonally striped border) surrounds the quilt on all sides. These two pieced borders are separated by a narrow, unpieced navy border.

Pieced Border 1

Step 1. Pin, then sew a 1½-inch navy strip to either side of a 4-inch muslin strip. Add a 3-inch muslin strip to one of the navy strips to complete a strip set, as shown in **Diagram 9.** Press the seam allowances toward the navy strips. Square up one end of the strip set, and cut twelve 2¾-inch segments from the strip set, as shown. Label these segments Unit 2.

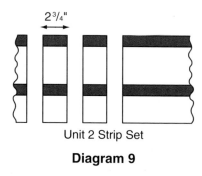

2¾"

Unit 2 Strip Set

Diagram 9

Step 2. Join six Unit 2 segments side by side, as shown in **Diagram 10.** Press the seams toward the navy strips. Make two of these border strips for the quilt sides.

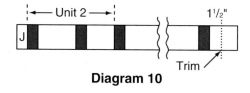

◄— Unit 2 —►   1½"

J

Trim

Diagram 10

Step 3. Trim the last muslin segment on the *right* end of each border strip so that it is 1½ inches wide. Sew a 1¾ × 2¾-inch muslin J piece to the left end of each border strip, as shown in the diagram. Press the seams toward the navy strips. Set the two Pieced Border 1 units aside.

Pieced Border 2

Step 1. Sew together a 2½-inch muslin strip, a 1¼-inch navy strip, a 3-inch dusty solid strip, and a 1¼-inch navy strip side by side, staggering their starting points by a distance equal to the strip width, as shown in **Diagram 11.** Make five such strip sets.

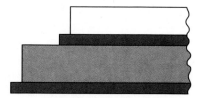

Diagram 11

Step 2. Align the 45 degree line of your rotary ruler with the seam line between the muslin and navy strips, as shown in **Diagram 12.** Use a rotary cutter to trim the end of the strip set, as shown. Realign your ruler so that the diagonal edge of the fabric is aligned with the 3½-inch line on the ruler and the 45 degree line is still in line with the seam of the strip set. Now cut a 3½-inch diagonal section from the strip set. Cut 26 segments in this manner and label them Unit 3.

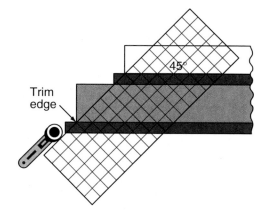

Trim edge

45°

Diagram 12

— Sew Easy

Because the Pieced Border 2 strips have the bias edges on the outside of the strips, be careful not to stretch the edges as you sew them to the quilt top. You may find it helpful to stay stitch the edges by machine stitching a scant ¼ inch from all raw edges. This extra step will keep your borders nice and even and prevent fabric-stretching headaches down the road.

Step 3. Sew six Unit 3 segments together, varying the colors, to make a top border. Repeat, making a bottom border in the same manner. Make two side borders in the same manner using seven Unit 3 segments in each border.

ADDING THE BORDERS

Step 1. Fold a Pieced Border 1 in half crosswise and crease. Unfold it and position it right side down along one side of the quilt top, with the crease at the quilt's midpoint. Pin at the midpoint and ends first, then along the entire length of the edge, easing in fullness if necessary. Sew the border to the quilt top, using a ¼-inch seam allowance. Press the seams toward the border. Repeat this procedure to add the remaining Pieced Border 1 to the opposite side of the quilt.

Step 2. You will need to piece two of the navy border strips so that they are long enough to fit the sides of the quilt top. Cut one of the navy border strips in half, and sew one half to two of the remaining navy border strips. Press the seams open. The top and bottom borders do not need to be pieced.

Step 3. Measure the quilt from side to side, taking the measurement through the center of the quilt, including the pieced borders. Trim the two unpieced navy border strips to this length. Using the procedure described in Step 1, sew a border strip to the top and bottom of the quilt. Press the seam allowances toward the navy strip.

Step 4. Measure the length of the quilt, taking the measurement through the center of the quilt and including the navy borders. Trim the remaining two navy border strips to this length. Stitch the borders to the quilt sides in the same manner as you did for the top and bottom borders. Press the seams toward the navy borders.

Step 5. Position a Pieced Border 2 along the top edge of the quilt top, with right sides together and the navy pieces aligned with the navy chimneys in the blocks. Pin the border in place, with the ends of the border extending beyond the edge of the

quilt top. Use a rotary cutter and ruler to square up the *left* edge of the strip. The strip should overhang the right edge of the quilt top by at least 3¼ inches, as shown. *Do not square up the right edge of the strip yet!* With the wrong side of the quilt top facing you, sew the border to the quilt top, using a ¼-inch seam. By having the border on the bottom as you sew, the bias edges of the border will be eased in to fit the quilt top by the feed dogs. Stop sewing approximately 3 inches from the edge of the quilt top and backstitch. Leave the end of the border strip free. Open out the border and press. See **Diagram 13**.

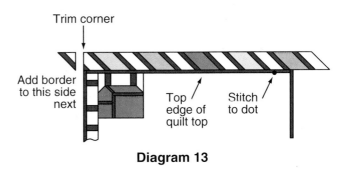

Diagram 13

Step 6. Attach the left border next, aligning the diagonal navy pieces in Pieced Border 2 with the navy strips in Pieced Border 1. The ends of the border will overhang the top and bottom edges of the quilt top slightly. Square up both ends of the border strip so they are even with the quilt top, and stitch the border in place.

Step 7. Attach the bottom border and then the right border in the same manner as you did for the top and left borders. To complete the quilt top, finish sewing the seam on the top border, and square up the right end of the border with the edge of the quilt top. Press the seams toward the border strips.

QUILTING AND FINISHING

Step 1. Mark the quilt top for quilting. The quilt shown is outline quilted around each shape with the exception of the navy strips, which are left unquilted.

Step 2. Cut the backing fabric in half crosswise. Remove the selvages and cut a 32-inch-wide panel from each piece. Sew the pieces together along the long edges. Press the seam open. The seam will run parallel to the top and bottom of the quilt. Refer to page 111 for more information on pieced backings.

Step 3. Layer the backing, batting, and quilt top and baste the layers together. Trim the excess backing and batting so they are approximately 3 inches larger than the quilt top on all sides. Quilt all marked designs, adding any additional quilting as desired.

Step 4. Referring to the directions on page 121, make and attach double-fold binding from the navy fabric. You will need approximately 205 inches of binding.

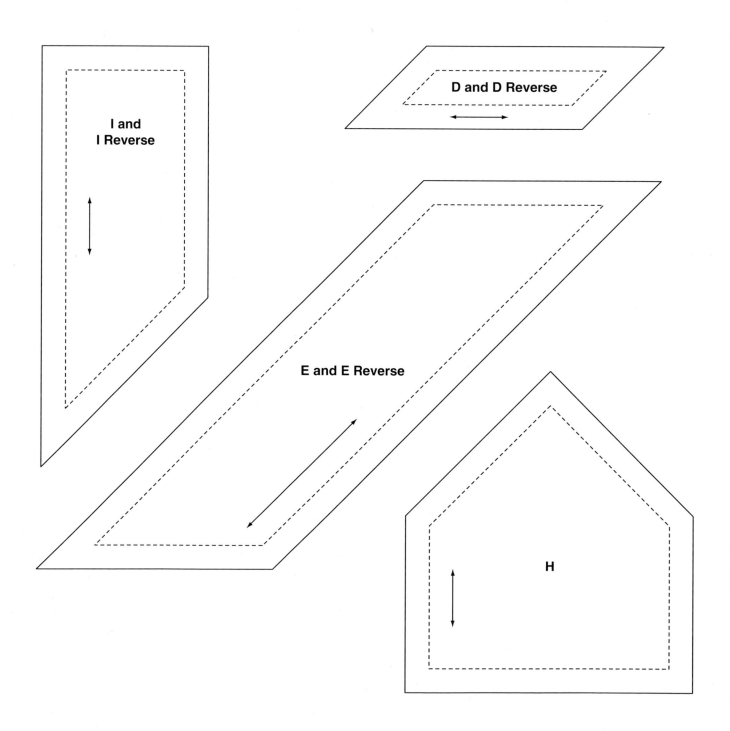

ROW HOUSES
Color Plan

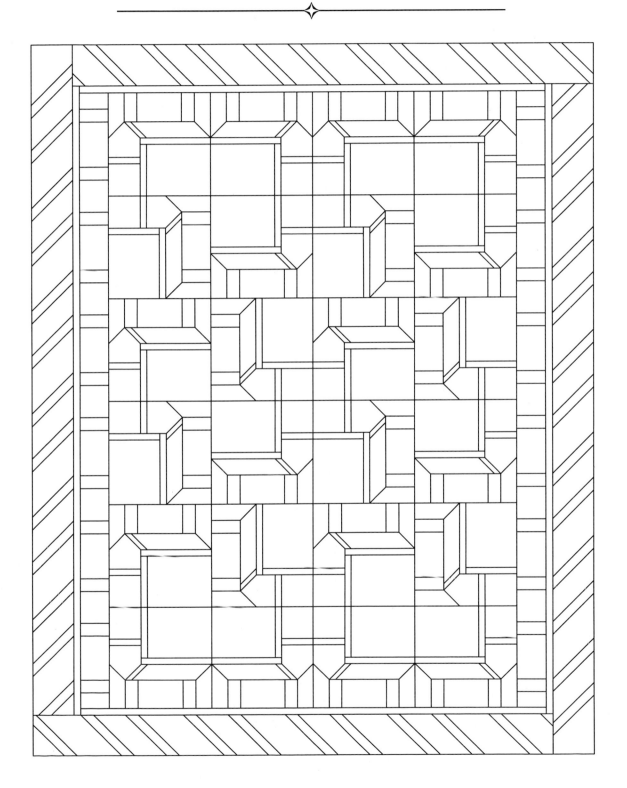

Photocopy this page and use it to experiment with color schemes for your quilt.

HOUSE MEDALLION

Skill Level: *Intermediate*

This quilt has a personality all its own, with its grab bag of striking, simple-to-piece borders. A carefree mix of brightly colored, boldly patterned stripes, checks, and polka dots lend Susan Bengston's original design a decidedly festive air. The generously sized lap quilt doubles as a cozy, bed-size coverlet or as a large wallhanging that will steal the spotlight in any family room or den.

————————————————◆————————————————

BEFORE YOU BEGIN

With its wide variety of fabrics and techniques, this quilt will give you the chance to try many things. It's rated intermediate simply because each successive border adds something new in terms of pattern or technique. The construction is simple enough, however, that a beginner can feel confident while broadening and sharpening her piecing skills.

Except for a few simple shapes that require templates, all of the pieces are strips, squares, and triangles that can be rotary cut. In addition, an easy strip-piecing technique is provided for making the checkerboard border.

Directions for two size variations are provided. The smaller wallhanging finishes with the first sawtooth border—a perfect size for a gift.

"Schoolhouse Basics," beginning on page 104, provides general information about making the Schoolhouse block, as well as for more details on rotary cutting and strip-piecing techniques.

CHOOSING FABRICS

The variety of modern polka dots, stripes, and checks com-

Quilt Sizes

	Wallhanging	Lap (shown)
Finished Quilt Size	36½" × 36½"	64" × 64"
Finished Block Size		
Schoolhouse	9"	9"
Star		6"
Number of Blocks		
Schoolhouse	4	4
Star		28

Materials

	Wallhanging	Lap
Red polka dot	¼ yard	⅝ yard
Red check	¼ yard	¼ yard
Assorted pink and red dots, stripes, and checks	⅓ yard	⅝ yard
Assorted tan, brown, and black dots, stripes, and checks	¾ yard	1⅞ yards
Brown-on-tan dots		¾ yard
Tan stripe	⅝ yard	¾ yard
Black solid	⅛ yard	¼ yard
Gold solid	⅛ yard	¼ yard
Tan and brown solids	⅛ yard	⅛ yard
Assorted bright dots, stripes, and checks	½ yard	1¾ yards
Backing	1¼ yards	4 yards
Batting	43" × 43"	70" × 70"

NOTE: Yardages are based on 44/45-inch-wide fabrics that are at least 42 inches wide after preshrinking.

Cutting Chart

Fabric	Used For	Strip Width	Number to Cut		Second Cut Dimensions
			Wallhanging	Lap	
Red polka dot	Border 1	2½"	2	2	
	Border 3	2"		6	
Red check	Border 2	1½"	4	4	
Pinks and reds	Sawtooth borders	2⅞"	3	6	2⅞" squares
Assorted tans, browns, and blacks	Checkerboard border	2"	4	4	
	Sawtooth borders	2⅞"	3	6	2⅞" squares
	Stars	2⅜"		1	2⅜" squares
	Stars	3½"		1	3½" squares
	On-point border	5½"		4	5½" squares
	On-point border	3"		1	3" squares
Black solid	Stars	4¼"		1	4¼" squares
	Stars	2"		1	2" squares
Brown-on-tan dots	Stars	4¼"		3	4¼" squares
	Stars	2"		5	2" squares
Brights	Checkerboard border	2"	8	8	
	Stars	2⅜"		6	2⅜" squares
	Stars	3½"		2	3½" squares
	On-point border	3½"		5	3½" squares

From the assorted tan, brown, and black prints and black and gold solids, cut the following pieces for each of the four Schoolhouse blocks. Refer to the *Schoolhouse Block Diagram* and the photograph on page 58 as needed.

Fabric	Used For	Dimensions	Number to Cut per House
House print 1	A	2" × 5"	2
	C	1½" × 5"	1
	H	Template H	1
House print 2	F	1½" × 4"	2
	D	1¼" × 4"	1
	G	1½" × 5"	2
Roof print	I	Template I	1
	K	1½" × 1½"	2
Door and window solid	B	2" × 5"	1
	E	1⅜" × 4"	2
Sky solid	L	1½" × 3"	1
	J and J reverse	Template J	1 each

plements the eclectic mix of traditional quilt block patterns in this happy-go-lucky quilt. The prints are from a single fabric line, so they coordinate effortlessly, which brings order to what might have been an otherwise dizzying array.

Brights, primaries, and jewel tones work especially well in this design. Neutrals such as tan, brown, and black add a calming influence. You might choose to work strictly in dots and geometrics or to add other prints and patterns. Draw

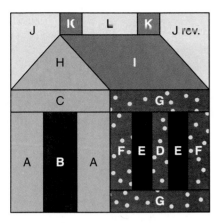

Schoolhouse Block Diagram

Cut sizes

A = 2" × 5"
B = 2" × 5"
C = 1½" × 5"
D = 1¼" × 4"
E = 1⅜" × 4"
F = 1½" × 4"
G = 1½" × 5"
K = 1½" × 1½"
L = 1½" × 3"

your selection from one fabric line or rely on a mixture from your scrap bag.

To develop a unique color scheme for the quilt, photocopy the **Color Plan** on page 67, and use crayons or colored pencils to experiment with different color arrangements.

CUTTING

All measurements include ¼-inch seam allowances. Refer to the Cutting Chart and cut the required number of strips and squares in the sizes needed. Cut all strips across the fabric width.

Make templates for pieces H, I, and J, using the full-size pattern pieces on page 66. Refer to page 116 for complete details on making and using templates. The Cutting Chart indicates how many of each piece to cut with each template. Place the templates wrong side up on the wrong side of the fabric to cut pieces, except for J reverse. Turn the J template over to cut piece J reverse.

You will need to cut some of the squares into triangles, as follows:

• For the Sawtooth borders, cut the 2⅞-inch assorted red, pink, tan, and brown squares in half diagonally, as shown in **Diagram 1A**. You'll need 68 red and pink triangles and 68 tan and brown triangles for the wallhanging. You'll need 168 red and pink and 168 brown and tan triangles for the lap quilt.

• For the bright Stars, cut the 4¼-inch brown-on-tan dot squares diagonally in half in each direction to make 96 triangles, as shown in **1B**. Cut the 2⅜-inch assorted bright squares in half once diagonally to make 192 triangles.

• For the dark Stars, cut the 2⅜-inch black and brown print squares in half diagonally to make 32 triangles. Cut the 4¼-inch black solid squares diagonally each way to make 16 triangles.

• For the on-point borders, cut the 5½-inch tan and brown squares diagonally in both directions to make 104 Y triangles. Cut the 3-inch tan and brown squares in half diagonally to make 16 Z triangles.

Note: Cut and piece a sample Schoolhouse and Star block before cutting fabric for all of the blocks in the quilt.

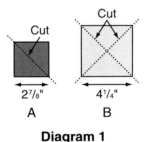

Diagram 1

ASSEMBLING THE SCHOOLHOUSE BLOCKS

Refer to the **Schoolhouse Block Diagram** as you assemble each block. Each pattern piece is lettered in the alphabetical order in which it will be sewn. Cutting dimensions are also provided for pieces that are rotary cut. For either quilt size, you will need four Schoolhouse blocks. While the houses are made from different fabrics, each house uses four fabrics, as specified in the Cutting Chart.

Step 1. Sew an A piece to either side of a B piece along the long edges, then add a C piece to the top of the unit, as shown in **Diagram 2** on page 62. Press all seams to one side.

Step 2. Sew an E piece to either side of a D piece. Add an F piece to either end of the unit, referring to **Diagram 3** on page 62. Sew a G piece to the top and bottom of the unit, as shown. Press all seams to one side.

Diagram 2

Diagram 3

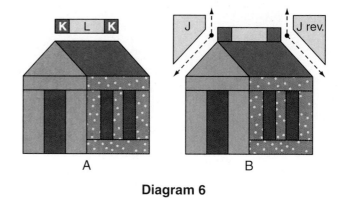

A

B

Diagram 6

Step 3. Join the two completed units. See **Diagram 4.** Press the seams toward the house front.

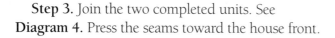

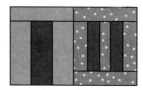

Diagram 4

Step 4. Sew an H piece to the left side of an I piece, as shown in **Diagram 5.** Press the seams toward I. Stitch this roof unit to the top edge of the house, as shown. Press the seams as desired and set aside.

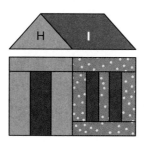

Diagram 5

Step 5. Sew a K piece to either side of an L piece, as shown in **Diagram 6A.** Press the seams away from L. Pin, then stitch this chimney unit to the top edge of the roof, as shown. Press the seams as desired. Set in the J and J reverse pieces, as shown in **6B.** For J, begin stitching ¼ inch from the raw edge at the point where H, I, and K meet. Attach J reverse in the same manner. In each case, stitch outward in the direction indicated by the arrows. Press the seams away from the J pieces. Refer to page 109 for additional information on set-in seams.

Step 6. Repeat Steps 1 through 5 to make a total of four Schoolhouse blocks.

Assembling the Quilt Center

Step 1. Use a design wall or other flat surface to lay out the four Schoolhouse blocks in two rows of two blocks each, as shown in the **Quilt Diagram.** Sew the blocks in horizontal rows, pressing the seam allowances in opposite directions from row to row. Sew the rows together, carefully matching seams. Press.

Step 2. Cut each of the 2-inch-wide red polka dot Border 1 strips in half to yield four strips that each measure approximately 21 inches long.

Step 3. Measure the four-block Schoolhouse unit from top to bottom, taking the measurement through the center, not along the sides. Trim two of the Border 1 strips to this length.

Step 4. Fold one strip in half crosswise and crease. Unfold it and position it right side down along one side of the four-block unit, with the midpoints and ends matching. Pin, easing in fullness if necessary. Sew the border to the quilt top, using a ¼-inch seam allowance. Press the seams toward the border strip. Repeat on the opposite side.

Step 5. Add the remaining border strips to the top and bottom edges of the quilt top in the same manner, except this time measure the quilt through its horizontal center and include the side borders.

Quilt Diagram

PIECING AND ADDING THE CHECKERBOARD BORDER

Step 1. Cut all of the 2-inch-wide strips for the checkerboard border in half so they are approximately 21 inches long. Sew the strips together in sets of three, referring to **Diagram 7.** The strips should contrast in value or color or both. Press the seams in one direction. Using a rotary cutter and ruler, square up one end of each strip set. Cut 2-inch-wide segments from the strip sets, as shown, until you have cut 68 segments.

Step 2. Sew the segments together, mixing fabrics and turning alternating segments so that adjoining seams are pressed in opposing directions. See **Diagram 8.** For either quilt, make two borders with 14 segments and two borders with 20 segments.

Step 3. Sew the 14-segment borders to the quilt sides, followed by the 20-segment top and bottom borders, matching the corner seams. Press seams toward the inner border. See "Sew Easy" on page 64 for tips on fitting pieced borders.

2"

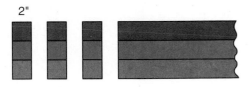

Diagram 7

Diagram 8

ADDING THE RED BORDER 2

Following the procedure described in Steps 3 and 4 of "Assembling the Quilt Center" on page 62, add the red side Border 2 strips, followed by the top and bottom Border 2 strips, to the quilt top. Refer to the **Quilt Diagram** on page 63.

MAKING AND ADDING THE SAWTOOTH BORDER

Step 1. Sew the red and pink triangles to the tan and brown triangles, as shown in **Diagram 9**, to make triangle squares. Make 68 for the wallhanging and 168 for the lap quilt. Press the seams toward the red and pink triangles.

Step 2. To make Sawtooth Border 1, sew the triangle-square units into strips, as shown in **Diagram 10**. Make two strips with 16 triangle squares each for the side borders and two strips with 18 triangle squares each for the top and bottom borders. Make sure that the triangle points change direction at middle of each border, as shown here and in the **Quilt Diagram** on page 63.

   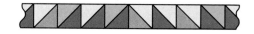

Diagram 9   **Diagram 10**

Step 3. Sew a Sawtooth Border 1 strip to each side of the quilt with the red and pink triangle edges aligned with the red check border. Press the seams toward the red check border. Add the top and bottom Sawtooth Border 1 strips in the same manner.

If you are making the wallhanging, proceed to "Quilting and Finishing" on page 66. If you are making the lap quilt, continue on with Step 4.

Step 4. The Sawtooth Border 2 is made exactly the same way as Sawtooth Border 1, except each side contains more triangle squares. You will need to make two strips with 24 triangle squares each for the side borders and two strips with 26 triangle squares each for the top and bottom borders. Again, be sure to change the direction of the

triangles at the midpoint of each border. Press the seams in one direction and set the borders aside.

——— Sew Easy ———

When joining two smaller triangles to a larger one, such as in the Star blocks, the resulting seams form an X. Stitch carefully through the center of the X when adding this pieced unit to the block for a perfect point where the two units meet.

The same principle holds true when piecing triangle squares into rows, as in the Sawtooth borders. Stitch through the X formed by the seams on the strip of triangle squares when attaching the border for more perfect points.

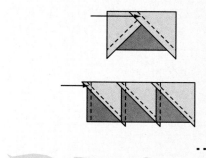

MAKING AND ADDING THE STAR BORDER

The blocks are all pieced in the same manner, as shown in the **Star Block Diagram**, but they are shaded in two different value arrangements. Make 24 blocks with brown-on-tan dots backgrounds, bright triangle points, and a contrasting center square. Make 4 blocks with black solid backgrounds, using a mix of black and tan prints for the points and centers.

Star Block Diagram

Step 1. Sew a bright triangle to each short side of a tan triangle, as shown in **Diagram 11A**. Press the seams toward the bright fabric. Make four identical units for each block. Sew a triangle unit to the top and bottom edge of a contrasting bright square, as shown. Press the seams toward the center square.

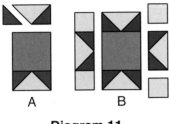

Diagram 11

Step 2. Sew a tan square to each end of the remaining two triangle units, as shown in **11B**. Press the seams toward the squares. Sew one of these strips to each side of the block. Press the seams as desired. Repeat to make 24 bright Star blocks.

Step 3. Make four dark Star blocks following Steps 1 and 2 above, substituting black solid for the tan polka dot pieces and black and tan polka dots and checks for the bright fabrics.

Step 4. Sew six bright Star blocks together in a row to make a border strip. Press the seams as desired. Make four of these border strips.

Step 5. Sew one border to each side of the quilt top, carefully matching the outer seams between the Star blocks with the seams of Sawtooth Border 1.

Step 6. Sew a dark Star block to each end of the remaining two bright Star borders, and sew these borders to the top and bottom edges of the quilt, matching seams. Press as desired.

ADDING SAWTOOTH BORDER 2

Referring to the **Quilt Diagram** on page 63, sew a Sawtooth Border 2 to each side of the quilt top in the same manner as for Sawtooth Border 1. Press, then repeat for the top and bottom of the quilt. Press.

ASSEMBLING AND ATTACHING THE FINAL BORDERS

Step 1. You will need to piece the red polka dot Border 3 strips to fit the quilt. Cut two of the strips in half crosswise and add a half strip to each of the remaining four strips.

Step 2. Add the borders in the same manner as for red Border 1 and 2. Add the side borders first, followed by the top and bottom borders. Press the seams toward the red borders.

Step 3. To assemble the on-point outer border, sew a tan or brown print Y triangle to two opposite sides of a 3½-inch bright print square, as shown in **Diagram 12A**. Press the seams toward the triangles. Make 48 of these units.

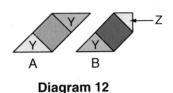

Diagram 12

Step 4. Sew Y and Z triangles to opposite sides of a bright print square, as shown in **12B**. Press the seam allowances toward the triangles. Make eight of these units.

Step 5. Sew 11 Y/square/Y units together to form a long border strip. Add a Y/square/Z unit to each end of the strip, and finish the strip by adding another Z triangle. See **Diagram 13**. Press the seams as desired. Make two of these border strips for the side borders.

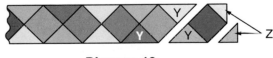

Diagram 13

Step 6. Make the top and bottom borders in the same manner, using 13 Y/square/Y units per strip.

Step 7. Sew the side borders to the quilt top, followed by the top and botton borders. Refer to the **Quilt Diagram.**

QUILTING AND FINISHING

Step 1. Mark the quilt top for quilting. The quilt shown is machine quilted in the ditch around most of the key shapes.

Step 2. For the lap quilt, you will need to piece the backing. Cut the backing fabric in half crosswise, and trim the selvages. Cut one piece in half lengthwise and sew one half to each side of the full-width piece. Press the seams away from the center panel. See page 111 for more information on pieced quilt backs. For the wallhanging, simply trim the selvages of the backing fabric.

Step 3. Layer the backing, batting, and quilt top; baste. Hand or machine quilt as desired.

Step 4. Referring to page 121, make and attach double-fold binding from the tan stripe fabric. Make about 154 inches for the wallhanging and 264 inches for the lap quilt.

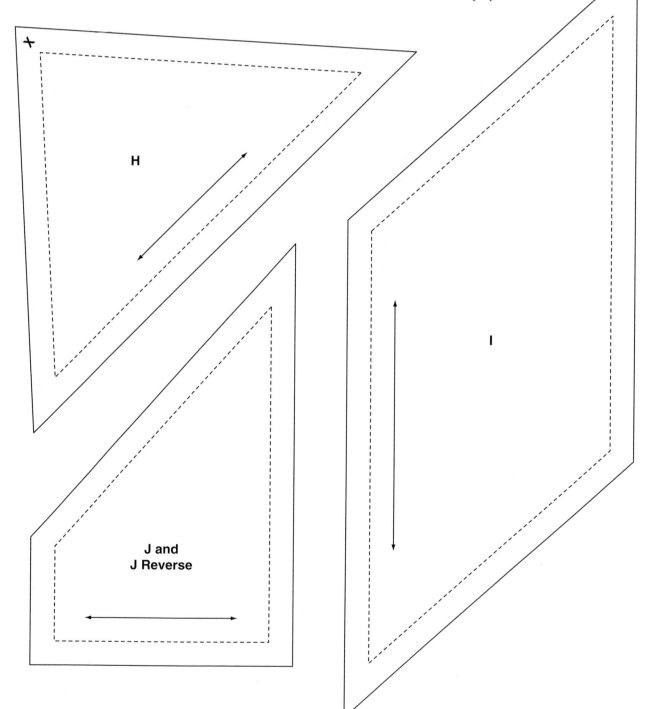

HOUSE MEDALLION
Color Plan

Photocopy this page and use it to experiment with color schemes for your quilt.

MY CABIN MADE OF LOGS

Skill Level: *Intermediate*

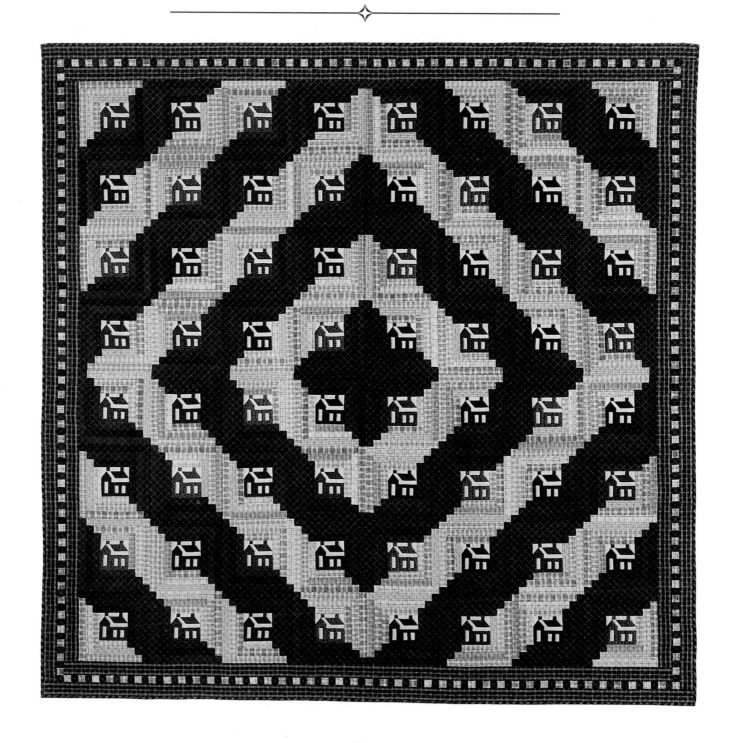

Quiltmaker Jane Graff developed the perfect recipe when she created this queen-size beauty that mixes two beloved designs—Schoolhouse and Log Cabin—to create a spectacular set. A popular homespun color scheme, a pieced border that makes efficient use of leftovers, plus favorite techniques like rotary cutting and strip piecing make this a quiltmaker's dream!

BEFORE YOU BEGIN

Although this design requires eight different block variations to achieve its clever barn raising setting, the construction of the quilt is actually quite easy. Just read the instructions carefully and refer often to the visuals provided, especially the photo, the **Schoolhouse Block Diagram** on page 71, the **Assembly Diagram** on page 74, and the **Quilt Diagram** on page 75. The latter will be particularly helpful as you position the various blocks to achieve the desired overall effect.

Two size variations are given: a generously sized queen, (as shown in the photograph), and a twin size. The twin size simply eliminates the outer ring of blocks, so the overall barn raising effect is not disturbed.

With the exception of a few simple shapes that require templates, all of the pieces are strips that can be rotary cut. A simple strip-piecing technique is provided for making the pieced border and parts of the Schoolhouse block, while chain piecing makes quick work of the Log Cabin blocks.

Quilt Sizes

	Twin	Queen (shown)
Finished Quilt Size	70½" × 70½"	90½" × 90½"
Finished Block Size		
Overall	10"	10"
Schoolhouse	4"	4"
Number of Blocks	36	36
Red Schoolhouses	18	32
Blue Schoolhouses	18	32
Variations 1, 4, 6, and 7	5 each	8 each
Variations 2, 3, 5, and 8	4 each	8 each

Materials

	Twin	Queen
Dark brown plaid	1⅞ yards	2⅛ yards
Tan solid	⅝ yard	⅞ yard
Assorted red prints	⅝ yard	⅞ yard
Assorted blue prints	⅝ yard	⅞ yard
Assorted light plaids, checks, and stripes	1⅞ yards	3¼ yards
Dark blue plaids, checks, and stripes	1⅛ yards	1⅞ yards
Dark red plaids, checks, and stripes	1⅛ yards	1⅞ yards
Backing	1¼ yards	8 yards
Batting	77" × 77"	97" × 97"

NOTE: Yardages are based on 44/45-inch-wide fabrics that are at least 42 inches wide after preshrinking.

69

Cutting Chart

Fabric	Used For	Strip Width or Piece	Number to Cut Twin	Number to Cut Queen	Second Cut Dimensions	Number to Cut Twin	Number to Cut Queen
Dark brown plaid	Inner borders	2½"	8	9			
	Outer borders	2½"	8	10			
Tan solids	Unit 2	2"	1	1			
	Unit 3	1"	2	4			
	Unit 1	1"	1	2			
	H	1"	3	5	1" × 3"	36	64
	B	Template B	36	64			
	D	Template D	36	64			
	D reverse	Template D	36	64			
Assorted red and blue prints*	Unit 2	1"	1	2			
	Unit 3	1"	2	2			
	Unit 1	1"	2	4			
	E	1"	2	4	1" × 2"	18	32 each
	F	1"	3	4	1" × 2"	18	32 each
	G	1"	2	2	1" × 2½"	18	32 each
	A	Template A	18	32			
	C	Template C	18	32			
Assorted light plaids and stripes	Pieced border	1½"	5	7			
Assorted red and blue plaids and stripes	Pieced border	1½"	5	7			

From the assorted red and blue prints, you will need to cut the quantity of strips or pieces listed from each of the prints (18 for twin or 32 for queen).

Fabric	Used For	Strip Width or Piece	Number to Cut Twin	Number to Cut Queen
Assorted light plaids and stripes	Logs	1½"	36	64
Assorted dark red plaids and stripes	Logs	1½"	22	37
Assorted dark blue plaids and stripes	Logs	1½"	22	37

Then, from the 1½" strips, cut the following pieces:

Fabric	Used For	Length of Log	Number of Logs Twin	Number of Logs Queen	Fabric	Used For	Length of Log	Number of Logs Twin	Number of Logs Queen
Assorted light plaids and stripes	Log 1	4½"	36	64	Assorted dark red and dark blue plaids and stripes	Log 3	5½"	18	32
	Log 2	5½"	36	64		Log 4	6½"	18	32
	Log 5	6½"	36	64		Log 7	7½"	18	32
	Log 6	7½"	36	64		Log 8	8½"	18	32
	Log 9	8½"	36	64		Log 11	9½"	18	32
	Log 10	9½"	36	64		Log 12	10½"	18	32

NOTE: *The "Number of Logs" is the total number to cut from each color group, not from each plaid.*

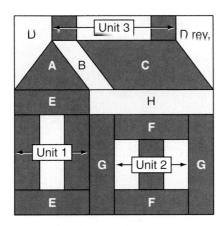

Schoolhouse Block Diagram

Before you begin, read through "Schoolhouse Basics," beginning on page 104, for more information about assembling the basic Schoolhouse block and for more details on strip-piecing and set-in piecing techniques.

CHOOSING FABRICS

This quilt lends itself to all kinds of fabric and color schemes. You can follow this quiltmaker's lead and use warm country reds, blues, beiges, and browns. As alternatives, consider rich reds and greens for a special holiday heirloom, soft pastels for a cabin in springtime look, or rainbow brights to please a child. You can make all of the Log Cabin blocks from the same six fabrics or utilize your scrap bag to make each block different.

The success of a Log Cabin design depends upon careful placement of light and dark fabrics. If you are working with a multitude of different fabrics, presort them into lights and darks. The lights don't need to be super light, just relatively lighter than the darks you pair with them.

To help develop your own unique color scheme for the quilt, photocopy the **Color Plan** on page 77, and use crayons or colored pencils to experiment with different color arrangements.

CUTTING

All of the measurements include ¼-inch seam allowances. Refer to the Cutting Chart and cut the required number of strips in the sizes

needed. Cut all strips across the fabric width (crosswise grain).

Make templates for pieces A, B, C, and D, using the full-size pattern pieces on page 76. Refer to page 116 for complete details on making and using templates. The Cutting Chart indicates how many of each piece to cut with each template. Place the B, C, and D templates right side up on the wrong side of the fabric to cut those pieces. Turn the D template over to cut the D reverse pieces. The A pattern is symmetrical, so it can be placed faceup or facedown.

Note: Cut and piece one sample block before cutting all the fabric for the quilt.

PIECING THE SCHOOLHOUSE BLOCKS

Refer to the **Schoolhouse Block Diagram** as you assemble each Schoolhouse block. Each pattern piece is identified by letter, and strip-pieced units are numbered. Refer to the Quilt Sizes chart on page 69 to determine the number of red and blue Schoolhouse blocks you will need for the quilt size you are making.

The Blue Schoolhouses

Step 1. Sew a 1-inch-wide blue strip to either side of a 1-inch-wide tan strip to form a strip set, as shown in **Diagram 1**. Press the seams toward the blue strips. Using a rotary cutter and ruler, square up one end of the strip set and cut 2-inch-wide segments from it, as shown. Label these segments Unit 1. Continue making strip sets and cutting them into segments until you have assembled one blue Unit 1 segment for each blue Schoolhouse block in your quilt.

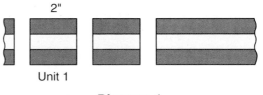

Unit 1

Diagram 1

Step 2. Sew a blue E along the top and bottom of each Unit 1, as shown in **Diagram 2** on page 72. Press the seams toward E. Set these units aside.

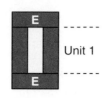

Diagram 2

Step 3. Sew a 1-inch tan strip to each side of a 1-inch blue strip. See **Diagram 3.** Press the seams toward the blue strip. Cut 1½-inch segments, as described in Step 1 on page 71. Continue making strip sets and cutting them into segments until you have one Unit 2 for each blue Schoolhouse block.

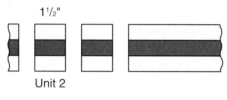

Diagram 3

Step 4. Sew a blue F along the top and bottom edges of each Unit 2, as shown in **Diagram 4.** Press the seams toward F. Then sew a blue G piece to each side of the unit, as shown. Press the seams toward G. Finally, add a tan H piece to the top of the unit, and press seams toward the blue fabric.

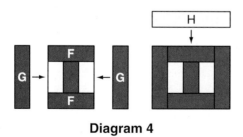

Diagram 4

Step 5. Join the two units, as shown in **Diagram 5,** to complete the base of the house. Press the seams toward Unit 2 and set aside.

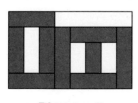

Diagram 5

Step 6. Sew a blue A piece, a tan B piece, and a blue C piece in sequence, as shown in **Diagram 6.** Press the seams toward the blue pieces. Stitch this roof unit to the top edge of the base of the house, as shown. Press the seams and set aside.

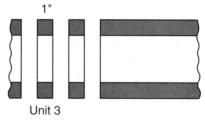

Diagram 6

Step 7. Sew a 1-inch-wide blue strip to either side of a 2-inch-wide tan strip to form a Unit 3 strip set, as shown in **Diagram 7.** Press the seams toward the blue strips. Cut 1-inch-wide segments. Continue making strip sets and cutting them into segments until you have one blue Unit 3 for each blue Schoolhouse block.

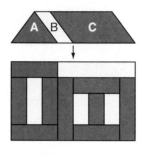

Diagram 7

Step 8. Sew a Unit 3 to the top edge of the house, as shown in **Diagram 8.** Begin and end stitching ¼ inch from the raw edges, as indicated by the dots. Press the seams toward the house.

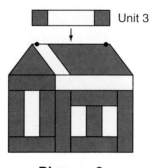

Diagram 8

Step 9. Set in the D and D reverse pieces, as shown in **Diagram 9.** For each piece, begin stitching ¼ inch from the raw edge at the base of the chimney (shown as dots on the diagram), and stitch outward in the direction indicated by the arrows. Press the seams toward the roof. Refer to page 109 for additional information on set-in seams.

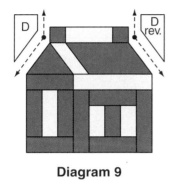

Diagram 9

The Red Schoolhouses

To construct the red Schoolhouse blocks, repeat Steps 1 through 9 under "The Blue Schoolhouses" on page 71, substituting red strips and pieces for the blue ones. Continue using tan pieces as directed for the blue Schoolhouse blocks.

COMPLETING THE LOG CABIN BLOCKS

There are eight block variations in this quilt. Each is pieced using the traditional log cabin method, with a light half and a dark half. Blocks 2, 4, 6, and 8 have a red schoolhouse as the center square. These blocks use blue strips for logs 3, 4, 11, and 12 and red strips for logs 7 and 8. All of the rest of the logs are light. Blocks 1, 3, 5, and 7 have a blue schoolhouse in the center. These blocks use red strips for logs 3, 4, 11, and 12 and blue strips for logs 7 and 8. The rest of the logs are light.

The only other difference between the blocks is where you start piecing with log 1. Use the labels on the **Log Cabin Blocks Diagram** for guidance in positioning log 1 and for the piecing order. Once log 1 has been sewn in place, the sewing procedure remains exactly the same for each variation.

Step 1. Attach each log by placing it right side down on top of the Schoolhouse block, aligning

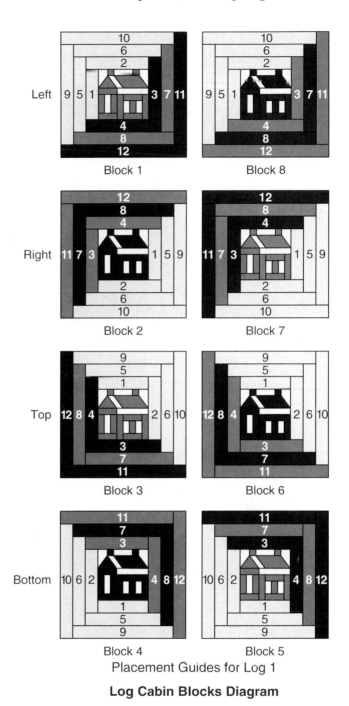

Placement Guides for Log 1

Log Cabin Blocks Diagram

the raw edges with the block edge to which it will be sewn. Press each seam away from the house before the next log is attached.

Step 2. Continue working your way around the block clockwise, adding logs in numerical order, as shown in **Diagram 10** on page 74. Refer to the Quilt Sizes chart on page 69 for the number of each block variation you will need for your quilt size.

Diagram 10

ASSEMBLING THE QUILT TOP

Step 1. Refer to the **Assembly Diagram** to lay out the quilt blocks. The twin-size quilt has six rows of six blocks each; the queen size has eight rows of eight blocks each. The **Assembly Diagram** is number coded to indicate which block variation should appear in each position in the quilt top. The heavy line inside the last ring of blocks indicates the layout for the twin-size quilt, while all of the blocks are required for the queen-size quilt. Refer to the photograph on page 68 for additional assistance.

Step 2. Sew the blocks together in horizontal rows, pressing the seams in opposite directions from row to row.

Step 3. Sew the rows together, carefully matching seams. Press as desired.

1	2	1	2	5	6	5	6
2	1	2	1	6	5	6	5
1	2	1	2	5	6	5	6
2	1	2	1	6	5	6	5
3	4	3	4	7	8	7	8
4	3	4	3	8	7	8	7
3	4	3	4	7	8	7	8
4	3	4	3	8	7	8	7

Assembly Diagram

Chain piecing is a real time-saver for constructing Log Cabin blocks. Pin and stack all like units that must be joined, such as the center Schoolhouse block and log 1. Begin sewing as usual, but do not backstitch or clip the thread between units. Continue to feed the units one after the other. Clip the connecting threads only after all of the units have been sewn. Press the seam allowances before proceeding to the next step. This method can be used to add each successive log to the blocks.

MAKING THE PIECED BORDER

Step 1. Make strip sets by sewing together pairs of 1½-inch-wide light plaids and stripes and assorted red and blue plaids and stripes. Press all seams toward the darker fabrics. See **Diagram 11**.

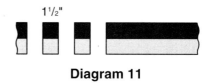

Diagram 11

Step 2. Using your rotary cutter and ruler, square up one end of a strip set and cut as many 1½-inch-wide segments as possible from it, as shown. Continue making and cutting strip sets until you have made 65 segments for the twin-size quilt or 85 segments for the queen size.

Step 3. Join the border units into strips, as shown in **Diagram 12**, alternating dark and light squares and mixing the fabrics as the strips are pieced. Press the seams toward the darker squares. For the twin size, you will need two strips of 32 units each for the side borders and two strips of 33 units each for the top and bottom borders. For the queen size, you will need two borders of 42 units each and two borders of 43 units each.

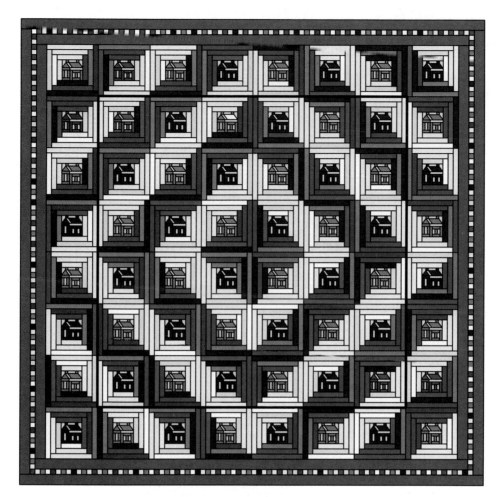

Quilt Diagram

Diagram 12

Adding the Borders

Refer to the **Quilt Diagram** as you assemble and attach the three borders to the quilt. The heavy line in the interior of the **Quilt Diagram** indicates the size of the twin-size quilt before borders are added.

Step 1. For either size quilt, you will need to piece the inner plaid borders to achieve the necessary length. For the twin-size quilt, sew four 2½-inch-wide dark plaid strips into pairs to form two long borders for the top and bottom of the quilt. Press the seams as desired. Cut one of the re-

maining 2½-inch-wide dark brown plaid strips in half, and sew one half to each of the remaining two strips to make the side borders.

For the queen-size quilt, sew the eight 2½-inch-wide dark brown plaid strips together into pairs to form four long border strips.

Step 2. Measure the quilt from top to bottom, taking the measurement through the center of the quilt, not along the sides. Trim the inner plaid side border strips to this length.

Step 3. Fold one trimmed side border in half crosswise and crease. Unfold it and position it right side down along one side of the quilt, with the crease at the quilt's horizontal midpoint. Pin at the midpoint and ends first, then along the length of the entire side, easing in fullness if necessary.

Sew the border to the quilt top, using a ¼-inch seam allowance. Press the seams toward the border. Repeat on the opposite side.

Step 4. Measure the width of the quilt, taking the measurement through the center of the quilt, including the side borders. Trim the top and bottom inner plaid borders to this length. Add the top and bottom borders to the quilt in the same manner as for the side borders.

Step 5. Position and pin a side pieced border strip to one side of the quilt top. Match the mid-points and ends first, and ease in fullness if necessary. Sew the border to the quilt, using a ¼-inch seam allowance. Press the seams toward the dark plaid border. Repeat on the opposite side. In the same manner, add the remaining pieced border strips to the top and bottom edges of the quilt.

Step 6. For either size quilt, piece the outer plaid borders to achieve the necessary length. For the twin-size quilt, join the eight 2½-inch-wide dark brown plaid strips into pairs to form four long border strips. For the queen size, join eight of the 2½-inch-wide dark brown plaid strips in pairs to form four long border strips. Cut the remaining two strips in half, and sew a half to each border.

Step 7. Attach the outer borders in the same manner as the inner borders. Add the side borders first, followed by the top and bottom borders.

QUILTING AND FINISHING

Step 1. Mark the quilt top for quilting. In the quilt shown, the house in each block is quilted in the ditch. The balance of the quilt is quilted in a crosshatch pattern of diagonal lines spaced ¾ inch apart.

Step 2. Regardless of which size quilt you're making, you'll need to piece the backing. For the twin-size quilt, cut the backing fabric in half crosswise, and trim the selvages. Cut one piece in half lengthwise and sew one half to each side of the full-width piece. Press the seams away from the center panel.

For the queen-size quilt, cut the backing fabric crosswise into three equal pieces, and trim the selvages. Sew the three pieces together along the long edges, pressing the seams away from the center panel. For either quilt, the backing seams will run parallel to the sides of the quilt. For more information on pieced quilt backs, see page 111.

Step 3. Layer the backing, batting, and quilt top, and baste. Quilt all marked designs, adding any additional quilting as desired.

Step 4. Referring to page 121, make and attach double-fold bias binding using the remaining dark plaid fabric. For the twin size, you will need approximately 290 inches of binding; for the queen size, you will need approximately 370 inches.

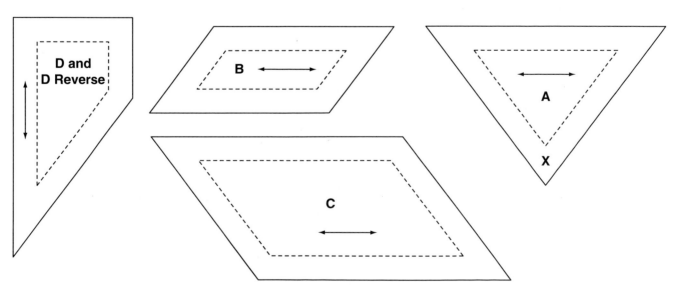

MY CABIN
MADE OF LOGS
Color Plan

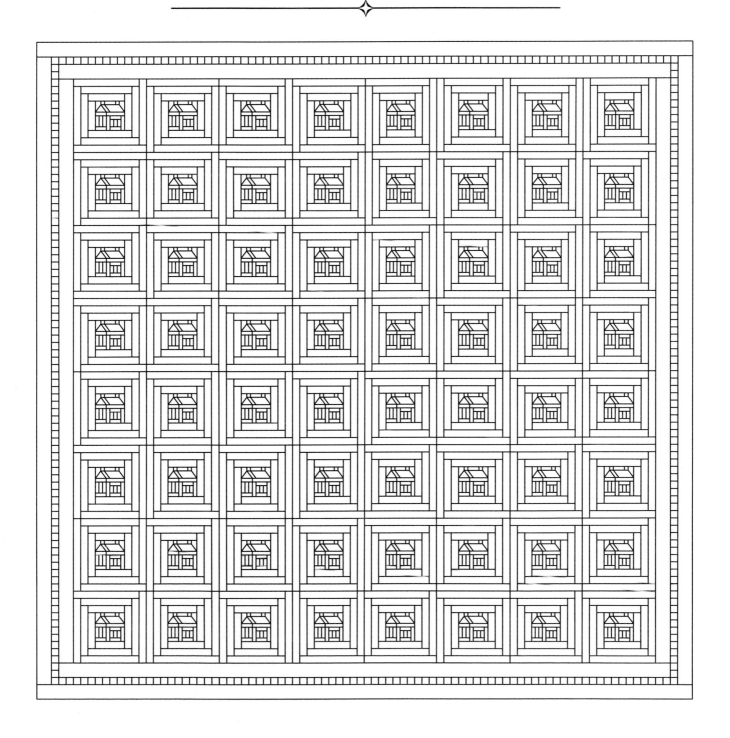

Photocopy this page and use it to experiment with color schemes for your quilt.

HONEYMOON COTTAGE

Skill Level: *Intermediate*

With its softly mellowed pastel colors and whimsical variation of the Schoolhouse theme, it seems likely that this lovely twin-size quilt dates back to the 1930s. The pattern name conjures pleasant images of optimism and romance—you can almost envision a youthful bride happily creating this future family heirloom.

BEFORE YOU BEGIN

Unlike the other quilts in this book, this Honeymoon Cottage block is rectangular, measuring wider than it is tall. The pattern is slightly modified to eliminate the need for set-in seams, reduce the number of oddly shaped pieces, and simplify the block's overall construction.

Several of the shapes require templates, but the remainder are strips and squares that can be rotary cut. In addition, easy strip piecing is used to assemble parts of the Honeymoon Cottage block.

Read through "Schoolhouse Basics," beginning on page 104, for additional information on strip piecing, as well as for helpful tips on piecing the Schoolhouse block and its many variations.

CHOOSING FABRICS

This quiltmaker's soft pastel palette was very fashionable in the era when the quilt was made. You might choose to maintain the period feeling by selecting a variety of solids in lavender, mint, buttercup, pink, and peach. Another option is to incorporate the many wonderful reproduction 1930s prints currently on the market. Or, for a totally different look, try clear crayon colors: red, green, blue, orange, yellow, and green.

To help develop a unique color scheme, photocopy the **Color Plan** on page 85, and use crayons or colored pencils to experiment with different color schemes.

Quilt Sizes		
	Twin (shown)	**Double**
Finished Quilt Size	70" × 76½"	86½" × 91"
Finished Block Size	11" × 13"	11" × 13"
Number of Blocks	20	30

Materials		
	Twin	**Double**
Muslin	1¼ yards	1¾ yards
Pale yellow solid	2⅞ yards	3¾ yards
Medium tan solid	¾ yard	1⅛ yards
Medium green solid	½ yard	¾ yard
Pink check	1⅛ yards	1½ yards
Black-and-white check	¼ yard	¼ yard
Bright yellow solid	½ yard	¾ yard
Backing	4¼ yards	7⅔ yards
Batting	76" × 83"	93" × 97"
Binding	⅝ yard	⅔ yard

NOTE: *Yardages are based on 44/45-inch-wide fabrics that are at least 42 inches wide after preshrinking.*

CUTTING

All of the measurements include ¼-inch seam allowances. Refer to the Cutting Chart on page 80 for the required number of strips in the sizes needed. Cut all strips across the fabric (crosswise grain).

Make templates for pieces A, B,

Cutting Chart

Fabric	Used For	Strip Width or Piece	Number to Cut Twin	Number to Cut Double	Second Cut Dimensions	Number to Cut Twin	Number to Cut Double
Muslin	Strip Set 1	1½"	2	2			
	Strip Set 2	1¾"	2	2			
	F	Template F	20	30			
	F reverse	Template F	20	30			
	I	3"	2	3	3" × 3¼"	20	30
	K	3"	5	8	3" × 9¼"	20	30
Pale yellow	Sashing strips	4"	17	24	4" × 11½"	25	36
					4" × 13½"	24	35
	Strip Set 1	1¾"	4	4			
	Strip Set 2	1¾"	6	6			
	D	Template D	20	30			
	D reverse	Template D	20	30			
Tan	E	Template E	20	30			
	G	Template G	20	30			
Green	A	Template A	20	30			
	C	Template C	20	30			
Pink check	Strip Set 1	3"	2	2			
	H	1⅜"	1	1	1⅜" × 1⅜"	20	30
	B	Template B	20	30			
	J	2"	4	5	2" × 6¼"	20	30
Black-and-white check	Strip Set 2	1½"	4	4			
Bright yellow	Sashing squares	4"	3	5	4" × 4"	30	42

C, D, E, F, and G, using the full-size pattern pieces on pages 83–84. Refer to page 116 for complete details on making and using templates. Place each of the templates wrong side up on the wrong side of the fabric and cut one A, B, C, D, E, F, and G piece for each block. Turn the D and F templates over to cut one D reverse and one F reverse piece for each block.

For the H triangles, cut the 1⅜-inch pink check squares in half diagonally, as shown in **Diagram 1.**

Note: Cut and piece one sample block before cutting all the fabric for the quilt.

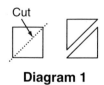

Cut

Diagram 1

PIECING THE COTTAGE BLOCKS

Refer to the **Block Diagram** as you assemble each block. For ease of construction, pieces are identified by their pattern piece letters. Strip-pieced units are numbered. Make 20 cottage blocks for the twin quilt and 30 cottage blocks for the double quilt.

Step 1. Sew a green A to the left side of a pink check B and a green C to the right side of B, as shown in **Diagram 2.** Press the seams away from B to complete Row 1 of the cottage block.

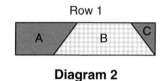

Row 1

A   B   C

Diagram 2

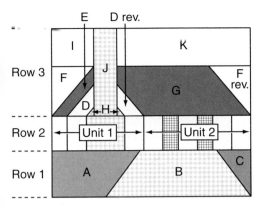

Cut sizes

I = 3" × 3¼"
J = 2" × 6½"
K = 3" × 9¼"

Block Diagram

Step 2. To make Strip Set 1 for the cottage front, sew a 1½-inch muslin strip, a 1¾-inch pale yellow strip, a 3-inch pink check strip, and a 1¾-inch pale yellow strip together side by side, as shown in **Diagram 3**. Press all seams to one side.

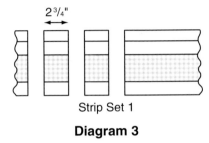

Strip Set 1

Diagram 3

Step 3. Using a rotary cutter and ruler, square up one end of the strip set. Cut 2¾-inch-wide Unit 1 segments from the strip set, as shown. Continue making strip sets and cutting segments until you have one Unit 1 segment for each cottage block.

Step 4. To make Strip Set 2, pin and sew together a 1¾-inch pale yellow strip, a 1½-inch black-and-white check strip, a 1¾-inch pale yellow strip, a 1½-inch black-and-white check strip, a 1¾-inch pale yellow strip, and a 1¾-inch muslin strip, as shown in **Diagram 4**. Press all seams to one side.

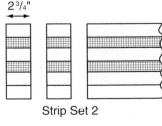

Strip Set 2

Diagram 4

Step 5. Square up one end of the strip set and cut 2¾-inch Unit 2 segments from the strip set, as shown. Continue making strip sets and cutting segments until you have one Unit 2 segment for each cottage block.

Step 6. Join Unit 1 and Unit 2, as shown in **Diagram 5**, to complete Row 2. Press the seams toward Unit 1 and set aside.

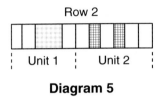

Row 2

Unit 1   Unit 2

Diagram 5

Step 7. For Row 3, sew a pale yellow D to one side of a tan E, then sew a muslin F to the other side of E, as shown in **Diagram 6A**. Press the seams toward E. Then add a pink check H triangle to the short edge of D, as shown. Press the seams toward D. Add a muslin I rectangle along the top edge of the pieced rectangle, as shown in **6B**. Press the seams toward I and set aside.

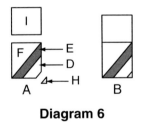

Diagram 6

Step 8. Sew a muslin D reverse and F reverse to either side a tan G, as shown in **Diagram 7**, pressing the seams toward G. Join a pink check H triangle to the short edge of D reverse, as shown. Press the seams toward D reverse. Add a muslin K strip along the top edge of the pieced roof unit. Press the seams toward K.

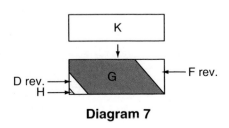

Diagram 7

Step 9. Sew the two pieced rectangles to either side of a pink check J strip. See **Diagram 8.** This completes Row 3. Press the seams toward J.

Row 3

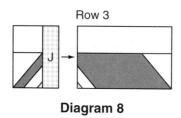

Diagram 8

Step 10. Join Rows 1, 2, and 3, matching appropriate seams, to complete one cottage block. Press as desired. Repeat all steps to complete the required number of blocks for your quilt size.

ASSEMBLING THE QUILT TOP

Step 1. Referring to the **Partial Twin-Size Assembly Diagram,** lay out the cottage blocks, the sashing strips, and the sashing squares. The quilt shown in the photograph on page 78 is the twin size. For the double size, you'll have six horizontal rows of five blocks each, as shown in the **Quilt Diagram.** Note that the 13½-inch strips form the horizontal sashing, while the 11½-inch strips form the vertical sashing between the cottage blocks.

Step 2. Sew the sashing squares and horizontal sashing strips together into rows, then sew the cottage blocks and vertical sashing strips into rows, as shown in the **Partial Twin-Size Assembly Diagram.** Press the seams in opposite directions from row to row.

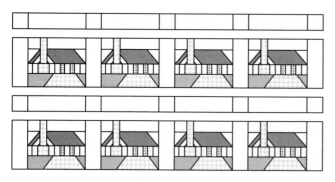

Partial Twin-Size Assembly Diagram

Step 3. Sew the rows together, carefully matching seams. Press.

QUILTING AND FINISHING

Step 1. Mark the quilt top for quilting. The quilt shown is quilted in an overall pattern of diagonal lines, stitched approximately 1 inch apart.

········Sew Quick········

To mark grid quilting lines, as in the quilt shown, use masking tape in the width desired for your grid. Position a strip of tape on the quilt top and quilt on either side of it. Then peel off the tape, reposition it along one of the quilted lines, and quilt along the other side of the tape. One strip of tape can be used several times before it loses its stickiness. When you're through quilting, you'll have no lines to erase!

Step 2. Regardless of which size quilt you're making, you'll have to piece the backing. For the twin quilt, cut the backing fabric in half crosswise, and trim the selvages. Cut one of the pieces in half lengthwise and sew one half to each side of the full-width piece. Press the seams toward the sides.

For the double quilt, cut the backing fabric crosswise into three equal pieces, and trim the selvages. Sew the pieces together along their long edges. Press the seams away from the center panel. The seams will run parallel to the top and bottom edges of the quilt. For more information on pieced quilt backs, see page 111.

Step 3. Layer the backing, batting, and quilt top, and baste. Quilt all marked designs.

Step 4. Referring to the directions on page 121, make and attach double-fold binding. You will need approximately 300 inches for the twin size and 363 inches for the double quilt.

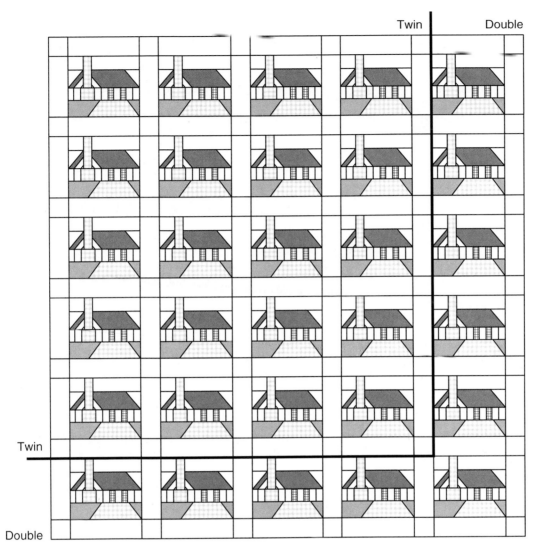

Quilt Diagram

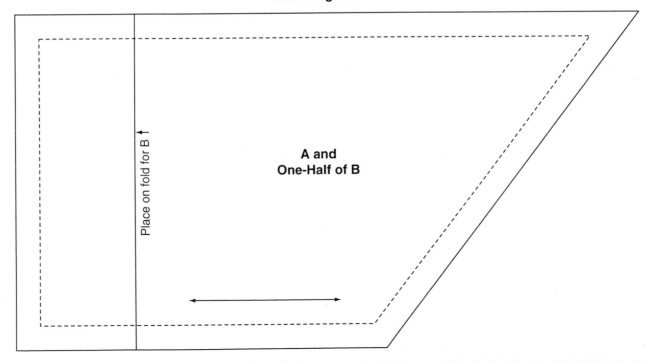

Place on fold for B

**A and
One-Half of B**

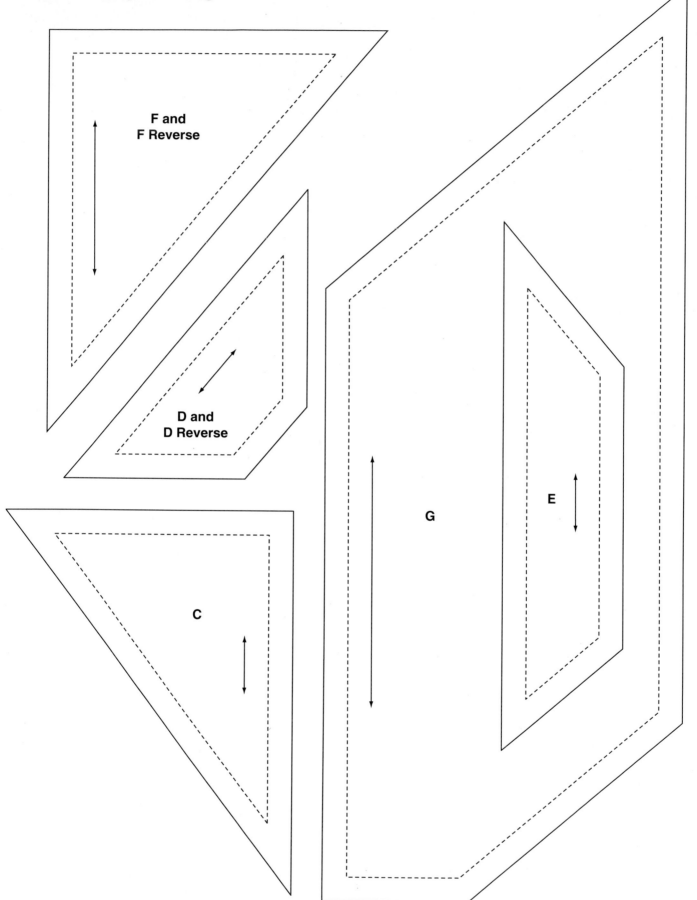

HONEYMOON COTTAGE
Color Plan

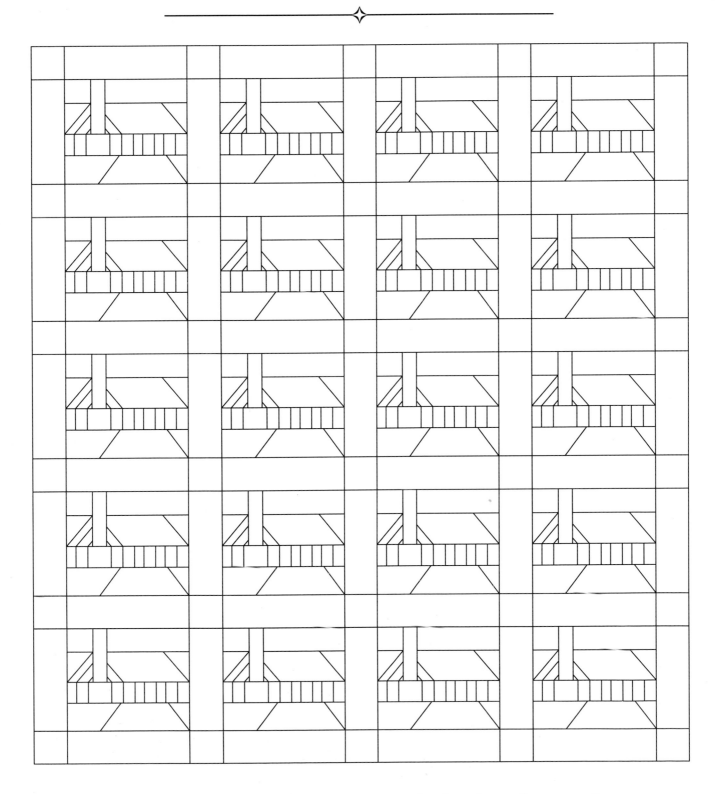

Photocopy this page and use it to experiment with color schemes for your quilt.

Memories of SS #3

Skill Level: *Intermediate*

The humble Schoolhouse simply glows in Doreen Hugill's colorful mix of madras plaids, charming homespuns, jewel-tone brights, and delicious hand-dyed fabrics. Carefully shaded sashing strips and diagonally cut borders add excitement and motion to this color-splashed wallhanging.

BEFORE YOU BEGIN

Since each Schoolhouse block in this quilt is pieced from a different combination of fabrics, strip piecing is not especially efficient. However, quick cutting is employed to speed construction. With the exception of a few simple shapes that require templates, most of the pieces are strips, squares, and triangles that can be rotary cut. Fabrics can be layered for more efficient cutting.

CHOOSING FABRICS

In terms of color, just about anything goes in this exuberant design! The quiltmaker has fearlessly mixed fire engine red and magenta, teal and chartreuse, fuchsia and orange all in the same quilt. The colorful plaids and single star–studded background fabric pull it all together with great success.

The wonderful diagonal movement in the sashing and borders is created with a combination of subtly shaded and carefully graduated hand-dyed and printed fabrics. The sashing strips and squares grow progressively darker as they move from the upper right to the lower left

corner of the quilt. The diagonally pieced borders and binding intensify this effect. A design wall will come in handy to create a similar effect as you arrange the pieces for this quilt.

To help develop a unique color scheme, photocopy the **Color Plan** on page 93, and use crayons or colored pencils to experiment with different color arrangements.

Quilt Size

Finished Quilt Size	33¼" × 40"
Finished Block Size	6"
Number of Blocks	20

NOTE: In order to maintain the balanced proportions and specific value progressions in this quilt design, no variations in size or layout are provided.

Materials

	Amount
Assorted madras and homespun plaids	⅔ yard
Assorted bright and neutral prints	⅝ yard
Medium pink mottled solid	¼ yard
Medium rose mottled solid	⅓ yard
Dark red mottled solid	⅓ yard
Tan with navy star print	⅓ yard
Assorted neutral prints	¼ yard
Seven yellow and gold solids, graded from light to dark	⅛ yard each
Backing	1⅓ yards
Batting	40" × 46"

NOTE: Yardages are based on 44/45-inch-wide fabrics that are at least 42 inches wide after preshrinking.

87

Cutting Chart

Fabric	Used For	Strip Width	Number of Strips	Second Cut Dimensions	Number to Cut
Medium pink	Borders	3"	1		
	Binding	2½"	1		
Medium rose	Borders	3"	2		
	Binding	2½"	2		
Dark red	Borders	3"	2		
	Binding	2½"	2		
Gold 1 (lightest)	Sashing	1¼"		1¼" × 6½"	6
	Squares	1⅝"	1	1⅝" squares	5
Gold 2	Sashing	1¼"	1	1¼" × 6½"	6
	Squares	1⅝"	1	1⅝" squares	4
Gold 3	Sashing	1¼"	2	1¼" × 6½"	8
	Squares	1⅝"	1	1⅝" squares	5
Gold 4	Sashing	1¼"	2	1¼" × 6½"	9
	Squares	1⅝"	1	1⅝" squares	5
Gold 5	Sashing	1¼"	2	1¼" × 6½"	8
	Squares	1⅝"	1	1⅝" squares	5
Gold 6	Sashing	1¼"	1	1¼" × 6½"	6
	Squares	1⅝"	1	1⅝" squares	4
Gold 7	Sashing	1¼"	1	1¼" × 6½"	6
	Squares	1⅝"	1	1⅝" squares	5
Tan-and-navy print	K and K reverse	Template K		20 each	
	L	2"	1	1¼" × 2"	20
	N	1¾"	2	1¼" × 1¾"	4 each

Cut the following pieces for each Schoolhouse block. In each block, pieces B (door), F (windows), I (roof), and N (chimneys) may be cut from the same brights and neutrals, all different brights and neutrals, or any combination. Refer to the *Block Diagram* and the photograph on page 86 as needed.

Fabric	Used For	Dimensions	Number to Cut per House
Plaids	A	1¼" × 3"	3
	D	1" × 2¼"	3
	F	1" × 3½"	1
	G	1½" × 3½"	1
	J	Template J	1
Bright and neutral prints	B	1½" × 3"	1
	E	1¼" × 2¼"	2
	H	Template H	1
	M	1¼" × 1½"	2
Assorted neutral prints	C	1" × 3¾"	1
	I	Template I	1

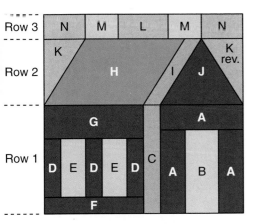

Row 3 | N M L M N
Row 2 | K H I J K rev.
Row 1 | G D E D E D C A A B A F

Block Diagram

Cut sizes

A = 1¼" × 3"
B = 1½" × 3"
C = 1" × 3¾"
D = 1" × 2¼"
E = 1¼" × 2¼"
F = 1" × 3½"
G = 1½" × 3½"
L = 1¼" × 2"
M = 1¼" × 1½"
N = 1¼" × 1¾"

CUTTING

All measurements include ¼-inch seam allowances. Refer to the Cutting Chart for the number of strips to cut in the sizes needed. Cut all strips across the fabric width (crosswise grain).

Make templates for pieces H, I, J, and K using the full-size pattern pieces on page 92. Refer to page 116 for complete details on making and using templates. The Cutting Chart indicates how many of each piece to cut with each template. Place the H, I, and K templates *wrong* side up on the wrong side of the fabric to cut those pieces. Turn the K template over to cut K reverse.

Cut each of the 1⅝-inch gold squares in half diagonally to make two triangles, as shown in **Diagram 1.** You will need nine triangles each from Gold 1, 3, 5, and 7; seven triangles from Gold 2 and 6; and ten triangles from Gold 4.

—— Sew Easy ——

It is not always easy to find just the right shades of fabric to show a slow progression of light-to-dark value such as in the sashing strips for this quilt. Sometimes the subtle difference in value from the front to the back of a fabric provides exactly the gradation you seek, so consider using the wrong side of some fabrics.

Note: Cut and piece one sample block before cutting all the fabric for the quilt.

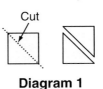

Cut

Diagram 1

PIECING THE SCHOOLHOUSE BLOCKS

Refer to the **Block Diagram** as you assemble each block. Each pattern piece is identified by a letter. For ease of construction, the pieces are lettered in the alphabetical order in which they will be sewn. Rotary-cutting dimensions are also given for pieces that do not require a template.

Step 1. Sew a house fabric A to either side of a window fabric B along the longest sides, and press the seams to one side. Then add another A piece to the top of the A/B/A unit, as shown in **Diagram 2.** Stitch a neutral C to the left of the entire unit, as shown. Press the seams toward the newly added strips, and set the unit aside.

Diagram 2

Step 2. Sew three house fabric D pieces to two window fabric E pieces along their longest sides, alternating fabrics in the sequence shown in **Diagram 3.** Press all seams to one side. Add a house fabric F along the bottom edge and a house fabric G along the top edge, as shown, pressing seams toward F and G.

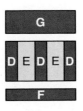

Diagram 3

Step 3. To complete Row 1, join the two units, as shown in **Diagram 4**. Press the seams toward C.

Row 1

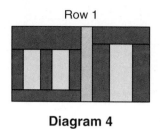

Diagram 4

Step 4. To make the roof section, sew an H, I, and J together, as shown in **Diagram 5**. Add a K and K reverse to either end of the roof, as shown. Press the seams as desired. This completes Row 2.

Row 2

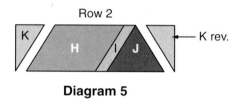
← K rev.

Diagram 5

Step 5. To make Row 3, sew an M chimney to either side of a tan L piece along the shortest sides. Add a tan N to each end of this unit, as shown in **Diagram 6**. Press the seams to one side.

Row 3

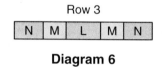

Diagram 6

Step 6. Referring to the **Block Diagram** on page 89, join Rows 1, 2, and 3 of the Schoolhouse block, carefully matching any appropriate seams. Press seams as desired.

ASSEMBLING THE QUILT TOP

Step 1. Refer to the **Assembly Diagram** and use a design wall or other flat surface to lay out the Schoolhouse blocks and sashing strips. The Schoolhouse blocks are arranged in five horizontal rows of four blocks each. The **Assembly Diagram** is coded to indicate where to place the various

yellow and gold sashing strips to achieve the desired progression from light to dark.

Step 2. Place the appropriately colored corner triangles to match the adjacent sashing strips to complete the color/value transitions, as shown in the **Assembly Diagram**. You may also find it helpful to refer to the photograph on page 86 as you lay out your quilt top.

Step 3. Sew each pair of corner triangles together along the diagonal seam to make the sashing squares. Press the seams toward the darker triangles. Note that in some cases the two triangles will be cut from the same shade of yellow or gold.

Step 4. Sew the pieced sashing squares and sashing strips together in horizontal rows. Stitch the Schoolhouse blocks and sashing strips in horizontal rows, as shown in the **Assembly Diagram**. Press the seams in opposite directions from row to row.

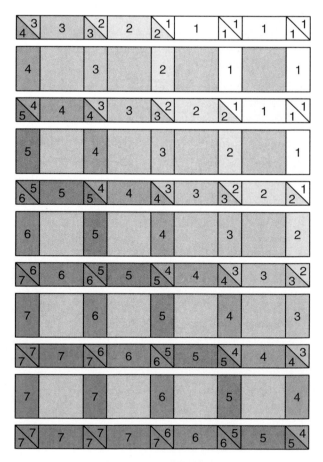

Assembly Diagram

Quilt Diagram

Step 5. Sew the rows together, carefully matching seams. Press as desired.

PIECING AND ADDING THE BORDERS

Step 1. Cut the pink border strip and one rose border strip in half to make two 21-inch-long strips of each. Cut the remaining rose border strip into a 12-inch and a 30-inch piece. Pair the border strips and label them as follows: 21-inch-rose and 21-inch pink—top; 30-inch rose and 21-inch pink—right; 42-inch red and 12-inch rose—bottom; and 42-inch red and 21-inch rose—left.

Step 2. Sew the pairs of strips together, angling the seams, as shown in **Diagram 7.** Press the seams toward the lighter strips.

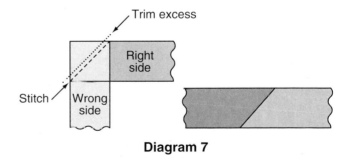

Diagram 7

Step 3. Sew the top and bottom borders to the quilt so the diagonal seams align with the diagonal seams in the sashing squares, as shown in the **Quilt Diagram.** Trim the borders even with the edges of the quilt top. Press the seams toward the borders.

Step 4. Sew the side borders to the quilt, positioning them so the diagonal seams align with the diagonal sashing square seams in the third row from the top. Trim the borders even with the quilt top, and press the seams toward the borders.

QUILTING AND FINISHING

Step 1. Mark the quilt top for quilting. The quilt shown is quilted in the ditch around the houses and along the sashing strips. The roof pieces are quilted to echo the pattern of the fabrics. The interior of the quilt top is quilted in randomly placed diagonal lines that run through the sashing strips, the block backgrounds, and the houses. Double parallel lines through the center of the border strips surround the entire quilt.

Step 2. Trim the selvages from the backing fabric. Layer the backing, batting, and quilt top; baste.

Step 3. Quilt all marked designs, adding any additional quilting as desired.

Step 4. The binding is pieced from the three border fabrics, and the seams are angled to correspond to and match the angles in the borders. Measure the perimeter of the quilt to determine where the binding will change color. Cut the binding strips to the appropriate lengths, leaving enough allowance on each strip so you can angle the seams in the same manner shown in **Diagram 7** on page 91 for the border strips. Attach the binding, aligning the angled seams, as shown in the photo on page 86. Refer to page 121 for additional instructions on making and attaching binding.

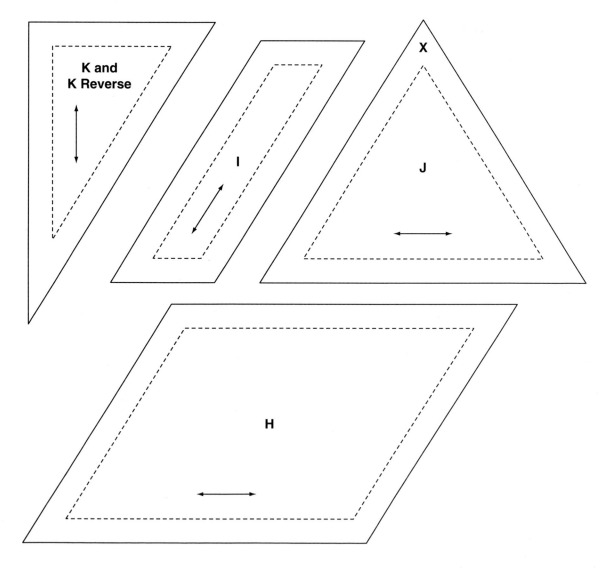

Color Plan

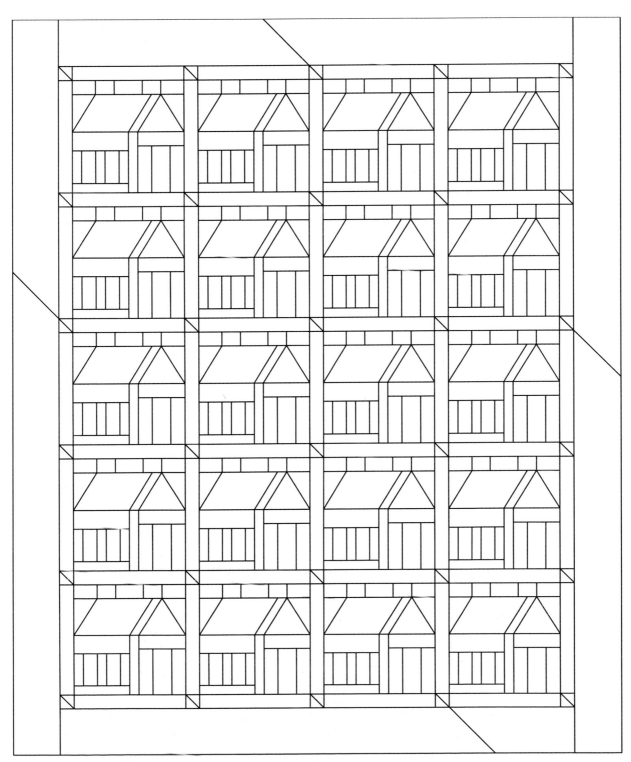

Photocopy this page and use it to experiment with color schemes for your quilt.

TEACHER OF THE YEAR

Skill Level: *Easy*

This cheerful twin-size quilt, with its strong colors, clever quilting motifs, and creative set, was designed for a favorite school-teacher, who just happened to be quiltmaker Miriam Dean's daughter! Large, simple shapes and easy strip piecing make sewing a snap, while the manageable size is perfect for that special teacher or young scholar in your life.

BEFORE YOU BEGIN

With the exception of a few simple shapes that require templates, all of the pieces are strips and squares that can be rotary cut. In addition, an easy strip-piecing technique is used to assemble large portions of each Schoolhouse block. These blocks go together very quickly and easily since there are no set-in seams.

"Schoolhouse Basics," beginning on page 104, contains more general information about constructing the Schoolhouse block, as well as more specific details on strip-piecing techniques.

CHOOSING FABRICS

This is a quilt that lends itself equally well to subtle prints, splashy textures, crayon-bright solids—or any combination! Making the blocks from the same fabrics, as this quiltmaker has done, enables you to use quick-cutting and strip-piecing techniques. The result is a crisp, visually striking design. If you don't mind sacrificing speed for variety, however, you might enjoy raiding your scrap bag to give each house its own fabric twist.

To develop a unique color scheme for the quilt, photocopy the **Color Plan** on page 103, and use colored pencils to experiment with different color arrangements.

Quilt Size	
Finished Quilt Size	60½" × 80½"
Finished Block Size	10"
Number of Blocks	
Schoolhouse	18
Apple	1
Block 1	12
Block 2	4

NOTE: Because the specific block arrangement is critical to the overall design of the quilt, no variations in size or layout are provided.

Materials	
Navy print	2 yards
Muslin	2⅞ yards
Red print	1⅔ yards
Dark green print	⅓ yard
Black subtle print	½ yard
Gray subtle print	⅛ yard
Backing	3¾ yards
Batting	66" × 86"

NOTE: Yardages are based on 44/45 inch-wide fabrics that are at least 42 inches wide after preshrinking.

CUTTING

All of the measurements include ¼-inch seam allowances. Refer to the Cutting Chart on page 96 and cut the required number of strips in the sizes

Fabric	Used For	Strip Width	Number of Strips	Second Cut Dimensions	Number to Cut
Navy print	Borders*	5½"	4		
	Block 1	10⅞"	1	10⅞" squares	6
	Block 2	11¼"	1	11¼" square	1
Muslin	Unit 1	2¾"	1		
	Unit 1	5¾"	1		
	Unit 2	3"	1		
	Units 3 and 5	1¼"	5		
	Unit 4	1¾"	2		
	A	Template A			18
	C	Template C			18
	E	Template E			18
	G	Template G			18
	G reverse	Template G			18
	J	1¼"	6	1¼" × 6¾"	36
	Block 1	10⅞"	3	10⅞" squares	8
	Block 2	11¼"	1	11¼" square	1
	Center square			10½" square	1
Red print	D	Template D			18
	H	1¼"	2	1¼" × 4½"	18
	I	1¼"	3	1¼" × 5¼"	18
	Unit 2	1¼"	2		
	Units 3 and 5	1¼"	5		
	Unit 4	1¼"	3		
	Apple	Apple template	1		
	Corner squares	5½"	1	5½" squares	4
Dark green	K	2"	5	2" × 10½"	18
	Leaf	Leaf template			1
Black print	B	Template B			18
	F	Template F			18
	Stem	Stem template			1
Gray print	Unit 1	3"	1		

Cut border strips on the lengthwise grain.

needed. Cut the navy print fabric first, cutting the border strips and strips for the large navy triangles along the lengthwise grain (parallel to the selvage). Cut the balance of the strips across the fabric width (crosswise grain).

Make templates for pieces A, B, C, D, E, F, and G, as well as for the apple, stem, and leaf appliqués, using the full-size pattern pieces on page 102. The templates, with the exception of the ap-

pliqué pieces, include ¼-inch seam allowances. Refer to page 116 for complete details on making and using templates.

The Cutting Chart indicates how many of each piece to cut with each template. Place the A, C, E, F, G, and Apple, Leaf, and Stem templates wrong side up on the wrong side of the fabric to cut those pieces.

Turn the G template over to cut G reverse. The

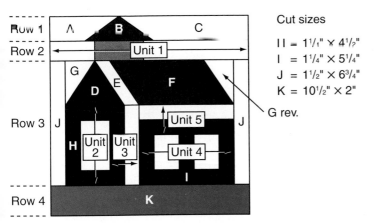

Schoolhouse Block Diagram

Cut sizes

H = 1¼" × 4½"
I = 1¼" × 5¼"
J = 1½" × 6¾"
K = 10½" × 2"

G rev.

B and D patterns are symmetrical, so they can be placed faceup or facedown.

Note: Cut and piece one sample block before cutting all the fabric for the quilt.

PIECING THE SCHOOLHOUSE BLOCKS

Refer to the **Schoolhouse Block Diagram** as you assemble each block. For ease of construction, each pattern piece is identified by letter, and strip-pieced units are numbered. You will need 18 Schoolhouse blocks for this quilt.

Step 1. Sew an A, B, and C piece together in sequence, as shown in **Diagram 1**, to complete Row 1 of the Schoolhouse block. Press the seams toward A and C. Repeat to make 18 rows, then set them aside.

Diagram 1

Step 2. To make Row 2, sew a 2¾-inch muslin strip, a 3-inch gray print strip, and a 5¾-inch muslin strip together side by side to form a Unit 1 strip set, as shown in **Diagram 2**. Press the seams toward the gray strip. Square up one end of the strip set and cut eighteen 1½-inch segments from it, as shown. Label these segments Row 2 and set them aside.

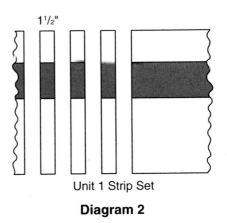

Unit 1 Strip Set
Diagram 2

Step 3. Row 3 is assembled in sections that are joined together before being attached to the other rows in the block. To make the house front section, sew a 1¼-inch red print strip to either side of a 3-inch muslin strip to form a Unit 2 strip set, as shown in **Diagram 3**. Press the seams toward the red strips. Using a rotary cutter and ruler, square up one end of the strip set and cut 18 Unit 2 segments, each 2 inches wide, as shown.

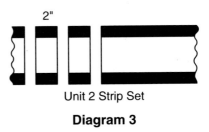

Unit 2 Strip Set
Diagram 3

Step 4. Sew together the 1¼-inch red print strips and the 1¼-inch muslin strips in pairs to form strip sets, as shown in **Diagram 4**. Press the seams toward the red strips. Square up one end of each strip set and cut 18 Unit 3 segments, each 4½ inches wide, as shown. Save the remaining strip sets for use in Step 7.

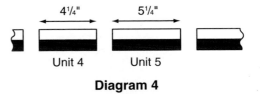

Diagram 4

Step 5. Referring to **Diagram 5** on page 98, sew a Unit 3 segment to the right edge of each

Unit 2 segment, so that the red strip in Unit 3 is attached to the edge of Unit 2 and the muslin strip is on the outer edge of the new unit. Sew a red print H along the left edge of Unit 2, as shown, to complete each house front. Press the seam allowances toward the red strips and set the units aside.

Diagram 5

Step 6. For the house side, pin then sew together three 1¼-inch red print strips and two 1¾-inch muslin strips, beginning with a red strip and alternating colors. See **Diagram 6.** Press the seams toward the red strips. Square up one end of the strip set and cut 18 Unit 4 segments, each 2¼ inches wide, as shown.

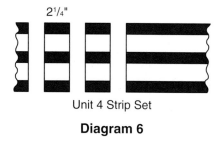

Unit 4 Strip Set

Diagram 6

Step 7. From the remaining red and muslin strip sets made in Step 4, cut eighteen 5¼-inch Unit 5 segments, as shown in **Diagram 4** on page 97.

Step 8. Sew the red edges of Unit 5 to the top edges of Unit 4. See **Diagram 7.** Then sew a red I to the bottom edge of each Unit 4, as shown. In each case, press the seams toward the red strips.

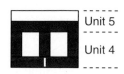

Diagram 7

Step 9. Sew together the house fronts and the house sides, as shown in **Diagram 8.** Press the seams toward the house front.

Diagram 8

Step 10. To make the roof of the house, sew D, E, F, G, and G reverse together in sequence, as shown in **Diagram 9.** Press the seams toward the darker pieces. Make 18 roof units, then sew them to the top of the houses, as shown. Press.

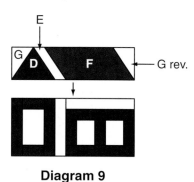

Diagram 9

Step 11. To complete Row 3, sew a muslin J to either side of the house units, as shown in **Diagram 10.** Then add a dark green K strip (Row 4) to the bottom edge of each house, as shown. Press all seams toward the new strips.

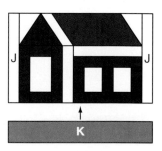

Diagram 10

Step 12. To complete the blocks, sew Rows 1 and 2 together, then sew them to the house tops. See the **Schoolhouse Block Diagram** on page 97.

APPLIQUÉING THE CENTER BLOCK

Use the appliqué method of your choice for the center Apple block. If you need more information about appliqué methods, see "Sew Easy" for specific details on the simple freezer paper appliqué method. Or see page 117 for additional information on needle-turn appliqué.

Step 1. Prepare a fabric apple, leaf, and stem for appliqué. Then fold the 10½-inch muslin center square in half vertically, horizontally, and diagonally both ways and crease lightly. Using the crease marks as a guide, place the stem, then the apple and leaf in the center of the block, referring to the photograph on page 94. The apple will overlap the bottom raw edge of the stem. Pin or baste all pieces in place.

Step 2. Using thread to match the appliqués and your favorite invisible stitch, appliqué the stem, apple, and leaf in place.

Sew Easy

The freezer paper appliqué method works especially well for shapes with lots of curves—such as the apple and leaf. The paper is a stabilizer, allowing you to turn seam allowances with ease.

Trace the *finished size* template onto the dull side of the freezer paper and cut out the paper shape directly on the pencil line. With a dry iron, press the freezer paper waxed side down on the wrong side of the appliqué fabric. Cut the fabric, adding a ³⁄₁₆-inch seam allowance around the paper shape. Roll the seam allowance over the dull side of the paper and baste it down, stitching through the paper.

Pin the shape to the background fabric and appliqué in place. Remove the basting stitches, make a small slit in the background fabric behind the appliquéd shape, and remove the freezer paper with tweezers.

Sew Quick

Add interest to your quilt with a bit of embroidery. Use two or three strands of dark brown or black embroidery thread and a simple stem or chain stitch to replace the appliqué apple stem. You'll add a touch of texture—and save time, too!

PIECING THE SETTING BLOCKS

There are two setting blocks that combine with the Schoolhouse and Apple blocks to give the quilt top its barn raising setting. Block 1 consists of a navy and muslin half-square triangle. Block 2 consists of a navy and muslin quarter-square triangle plus a muslin half-square triangle. Refer to the **Setting Blocks Diagram** as you work.

Block 1   Block 2
Setting Blocks Diagram

Block 1

Step 1. Cut six 10⅞-inch muslin squares in half diagonally, as shown in **Diagram 11A**, to make 12 triangles. Repeat with the six 10⅞-inch navy print squares.

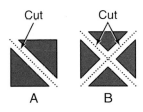
Diagram 11

Step 2. Sew a navy print triangle and a muslin triangle together along the diagonal edge to form a square, as shown in the **Setting Blocks Diagram**. Press the seams toward the navy triangle. Make 12 of these navy/muslin squares.

Block 2

Step 1. Cut the muslin and the navy 11¼-inch squares diagonally into quarters, as shown in **11B** on page 99. Sew a navy triangle to a muslin triangle along a short edge, as shown in the **Setting Blocks Diagram** on page 99. Repeat to make four sets of navy/muslin triangles. Press the seams toward the navy triangles.

Step 2. Cut the remaining two 10⅞-inch muslin squares in half diagonally, as you did for Block 1, to make four triangles.

Stitch the navy/muslin triangle to the large muslin triangle along the long edge to form a square. Press the seams toward the muslin triangle. Repeat to make four Block 2 setting blocks.

ASSEMBLING THE QUILT TOP

Step 1. Use a design wall or other flat surface to lay out the Apple block, the Schoolhouse blocks, and the Block 1 and Block 2 setting blocks in seven horizontal rows of five blocks each, referring to the **Assembly Diagram** for directional placement of Blocks 1 and 2.

Step 2. Sew the blocks together in horizontal rows, as shown. Press the seams in opposite directions from row to row.

Step 3. Sew the rows together, carefully matching seams where the blocks meet.

ADDING THE BORDER

Step 1. Measure the quilt from top to bottom, taking the measurement through the center of the quilt, not along the sides. Trim two of the borders to this length for side borders.

Step 2. Fold one side border in half crosswise and crease. Unfold it and position it right side down along one side of the quilt top, with the crease at the quilt's horizontal midpoint. Pin at the midpoint and ends first, then along the length of the entire side, easing in fullness if necessary. Sew the border to the quilt top, using a ¼-inch seam

Assembly Diagram

allowance. Press the seams toward the border. Repeat on the opposite side.

Step 3. Measure the width of the quilt, taking the measurement through the horizontal center of the quilt. Do not include the side borders in your measurement, but add ½ inch to your measurement for seam allowances. Trim the remaining two navy borders to this length. Sew a 5½-inch red print corner square to each end of both navy borders. Press the seams toward the navy borders.

Step 4. In the same manner as for the side borders, position and pin a border strip along the top edge of the quilt, matching seams and easing in fullness if necessary. Stitch the border to the quilt top. Repeat, adding the remaining border to the bottom edge of the quilt. Press the seams toward the borders. See the **Quilt Diagram.**

Quilt Diagram

QUILTING AND FINISHING

Step 1. Mark the quilt top for quilting. The Schoolhouse blocks in the quilt shown are quilted in the ditch, with a sun quilted in each upper right hand corner. The Apple block is outline quilted and has a crosshatched background. The navy triangles in Blocks 1 and 2 are quilted in concentric triangles. The muslin triangles are quilted with the letters of the alphabet, large numerals, paper doll–style children holding hands, and other whimsical motifs. The paper doll motif repeats in the borders, and each corner square has a quilted apple. Crayon-colored quilting thread (red, yellow, green, and blue) is used throughout.

Step 2. Cut the backing fabric in half crosswise, and trim the selvages. Cut one piece in half lengthwise and sew one half to each side of the full-width piece. The seams will run parallel to the top and bottom of the quilt top. Press the seams away from the center panel. For more information on pieced quilt backs, see page 111.

Step 3. Layer the backing, batting, and quilt top; baste. Quilt all marked designs, adding any additional quilting as desired.

Step 4. Referring to the directions on page 121, make and attach double-fold binding from the red print fabric. You will need approximately 290 inches of binding.

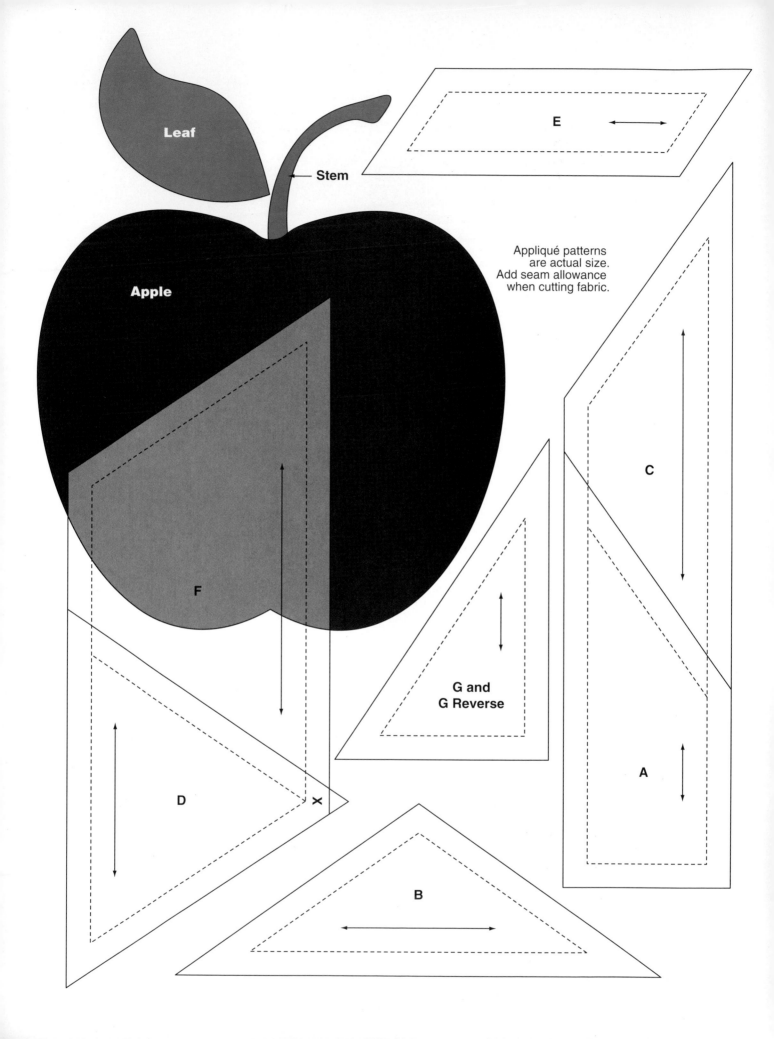

Leaf

Stem

Apple

Appliqué patterns
are actual size.
Add seam allowance
when cutting fabric.

E

C

F

G and
G Reverse

A

D

X

B

TEACHER OF THE YEAR
Color Plan

Photocopy this page and use it to experiment with color schemes for your quilt.

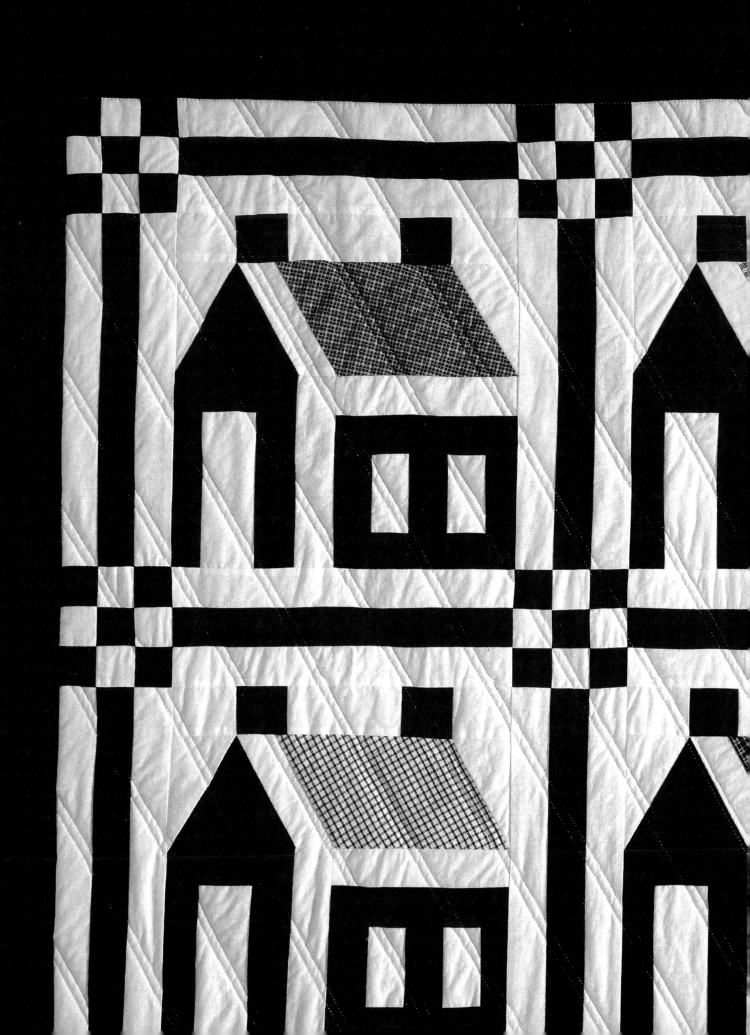

SCHOOLHOUSE
—◇—
BASICS

Using Schoolhouse Basics

The step-by-step instructions for many of the quilts in this book are based on a variety of quick-cutting and quick-piecing techniques. In this section, you'll find more specific details on these timesaving techniques, as well as helpful information relating to Schoolhouse quilts in general. We recommend that you read through this section before beginning any of the projects in the book.

Basic Block Characteristics

Although the motif has many variations, most house blocks share the same basic characteristics. Each is composed of a "ground floor," made up of a door, one or two windows, and the surrounding framework. This ground floor is topped with a gabled roof and finished with a skyline that includes one or two chimneys.

Many of the pieces are simple strips, making this block an ideal candidate for rotary cutting. When all or many of the blocks are pieced from the same fabrics, strip-piecing techniques make construction even more efficient.

Some of the house blocks can be pieced completely in rows. Others require an occasional set-in seam, as detailed on page 117.

Here are a few tips to help you with the construction of the typical house block.

• Carefully consider grain line when cutting the pieces for each block, as well as for setting triangles and squares. Straight grain refers to both the lengthwise and crosswise grain (or weave) of the fabric. Ideally, the straight of grain should run parallel to the outer edge of the block. The templates in this book have arrows to assist you with proper grain line placement. Instructions for rotary cutting strips, triangles, and squares consider grain line as well.

• If you study a Schoolhouse block carefully, you'll discover that some of the pieces, particularly some of those forming the roof and the skyline, must point in a specific direction in order for the block to fit together and face in the right direction when finished. Each project gives specific instructions as to whether to place your templates faceup or facedown to ensure that you have no backward pieces. **Note:** Some patterns are overlapped so they could be shown full size. Trace templates carefully.

• Depending on the design and proportion of the block, the triangle that forms the peak of the roofline may not be an equilateral triangle (equal on all sides). To avoid turning this triangle the wrong way when piecing it into the block, transfer the small X on the top point of the pattern to your template and fabric pieces.

• While taking an accurate $\frac{1}{4}$-inch seam allowance is essential in all piecing, it is especially so in a house block, where there may be as many as eight vertical seams across the ground floor row of the block. A variance as slight as $\frac{1}{16}$ inch per seam allowance can add up to a discrepancy of $\frac{1}{2}$ inch across the width of the block! Needless to say, this can lead to difficulty when the blocks are pieced together. To avoid frustration, be certain that your sewing machine is accurately marked for $\frac{1}{4}$-inch seams and be careful while sewing.

——— Sew Easy ———

Many newer sewing machines have a $\frac{1}{4}$-inch seam marking etched in the throat plate. Others have a presser foot that measures exactly $\frac{1}{4}$ inch wide. If your machine does not have a built-in guideline, check with your local quilt shop about a quilter's Little Foot attachment, which gauges an exact $\frac{1}{4}$-inch seam allowance and is available for most sewing machines. Or check with your sewing machine dealer to see if a $\frac{1}{4}$-inch foot is available for your machine.

Selecting Fabrics

When we think of the classic Schoolhouse quilt, we often think of a two-color arrangement combining white or unbleached muslin with a contrasting dark solid or print. While red—or possibly indigo blue—might seem like the most likely choices, these quilts are equally effective in any two-color combination that offers strong contrast between the house itself and the block background.

A two-color quilt can be composed of a single light and a single dark fabric, or it can include many fabrics from the color families of the light and dark that you have chosen. A Schoolhouse quilt can be worked in all solids, all prints, or in any combination of the two. Keep in mind that the background does not need to be the lighter of the two colors. Black can make a very dramatic backdrop for a Schoolhouse quilt.

If the idea of using two colors seems too limiting, feel free to experiment with a variety of color schemes. Look carefully at the photos of the quilts in this book, and you'll discover that the quiltmakers have designed quilts that range from two colors to those that include every color in the rainbow. In some, each block is identical to its neighbor; in others, no two blocks are alike. In fact, the Schoolhouse makes the ideal scrap quilt: No matter what the size of the block, the individual pieces are relatively small, so you can mix and match to your heart's content!

Whatever fabrics you choose for your quilt, be certain that there is enough contrast in value so that the house is distinguishable from the background and the doors and windows from the frame of the house itself. If you are using prints, look for a good mix. Include florals and vines, plaids and checks, dots and paisleys in both large and small scale to create the contrast necessary to establish the design of your quilt. The variety will make your quilt more interesting to see, as well as more fun to make!

USING A DESIGN WALL

A design wall can be a useful addition to your work space, allowing you to play with a variety of fabric and block arrangements before the actual blocks are sewn and set into a finished quilt top. It can be as simple or elaborate, temporary or permanent, large or small as your space and circumstances permit.

The ideal surface for a design wall is white cotton material such as batting, felt, or flannel. These cotton materials grip the cut fabric pieces and blocks, eliminating the need for pins. This allows you to "audition" any number of fabric arrangements and sets with ease.

Sew Easy

When choosing fabric for a design wall, be certain it is white. The choice of white, as opposed to any other color (or neutral), ensures that you are getting the truest possible reading in terms of color and value when placing other fabrics on the design surface. The background will stay unobtrusively in the background—where it belongs!

There are numerous other advantages to working with a design wall. A design wall enables you to maintain improved visual perspective on your developing work. When you view quilt blocks on the floor, the bed, or any other horizontal surface, the blocks farthest away tend to become visually distorted, appearing somewhat out of proportion. While this might be fine when the finished quilt is actually on the bed, it can cause some problems while the quilt is still in the design stage. Working on a vertical surface can help to eliminate this distortion.

In addition, a design wall allows you to step back from your quilt and view it from a distance, so you can get a better view of your fabrics in terms of their color, value, and visual texture and determine if they are serving the role you want them to play. A design wall can be invaluable in this respect. Here are some ideas for establishing a design wall in your work space.

• A design wall can be as simple as a square of white cotton batting, flannel, or felt taped or pinned to the wall. Choose the wall in your sewing room that affords you the greatest possible viewing distance and the largest square of fabric that your wall can accommodate. Two yards of white flannel, which is often sold 72 inches wide, makes an inexpensive and ideal design wall.

• For a portable design wall, staple a piece of felt or flannel over stetcher bars in a fashion similar to an artist's canvas. You can size this portable wall to your own personal needs, making it as large or as small as you wish. You can move it from room to room as necessary at home, and you can even take it with you to workshops and classes.

• If your work space can accommodate a more permanent arrangement, consider covering a sheet of Celotex with felt or flannel and affixing it securely to the workroom wall. Available at most building-supply stores, a Celotex wall has the added advantage of acting as a bulletin board. Sketches, photos, and fabrics can be tacked to the surface without harming the wall underneath.

Sew Quick

Using a temporary design wall but need to store the quilt layout until your next sewing session? If you have all of your quilt blocks or pieces laid out on a large piece of flannel but have run out of time to work on your quilt until a future date, try laying a large plastic trash bag (or two) over all of your quilt pieces. Pin the bag in place around the perimeter, and add a few pins to the central portion to hold it in place. Then you can fold or roll up the flannel and store it until your next sewing room session.

ROTARY-CUTTING BASICS

Whichever variation of the Schoolhouse block you choose to make, you will discover that many of the pieces are strips that can be rotary cut. Even if each block in the quilt is made from a different combination of fabrics and strip-piecing techniques do not apply, the rotary cutter can still be used to cut the individual pieces in the block, as well as any sashing and border strips. See page 115 for basic guidelines on rotary-cutting techniques.

STRIP-PIECING BASICS

Some of the blocks shown in this book are composed of a combination of miscellaneous shapes cut with traditional templates and strips and shapes cut with the rotary cutter. Sometimes the rotary-cut strips are assembled into groups, sewn together to make strips sets, and then cut apart into smaller units and segments. The piecing instructions for each quilt detail which strips to combine—and in which order—for each strip set in the quilt. Arrange the strips in order before you begin to sew.

Sew Easy

As you add each strip to make a strip set, begin sewing at the opposite end from where the previously sewn seam began. By sewing these long seams in alternate directions, you will eliminate much of the distortion that can occur when lengthy strips are joined.

Step 1. Align Strip 1 with Strip 2, placing right sides together and carefully matching the raw edges. Pin generously, then sew, taking care to maintain an accurate and consistent $\frac{1}{4}$-inch seam allowance. Add each additional strip in order until the strip set is complete, as shown in **Diagram 1.**

Diagram 1

Step 2. To press the strip set, work on one seam at a time. First set the seam by pressing it flat, just as it was sewn. Then open out one of the strips and gently press the seam from the right side, using an up-and-down motion with the iron. Do not slide your iron along the strips, as this movement can stretch your fabric. You will be simultaneously pressing both the strip and the seam allowance flat. If necessary, use your fingers to reach under the strip to guide the seam allowance. Repeat for each additional seam allowance.

Step 3. No matter how carefully you align the raw edges when piecing the strips, the ends of the strip set will probably be slightly uneven. To even the edges, place your see-through gridded ruler at one end of the strip set, as shown in **Diagram 2.** Carefully align a horizontal marking on the ruler with one of the seam lines. This will ensure that the cut edge is at a perfect 90 degree angle (perpendicular) to the seams in the strip set. Use a rotary cutter to cut across the entire width of the strip set, trimming away the uneven end.

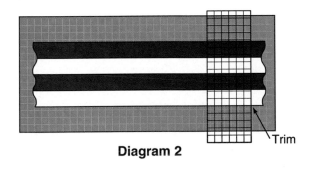
Diagram 2

Step 4. Refer to the Cutting Chart and the specific instructions for the quilt you are making to determine how many segments to cut from each set and how wide each segment needs to be. Use your rotary cutter and gridded ruler to cut the appropriate number of segments in the desired widths. Be sure to maintain the 90 degree edge by keeping a horizontal line on the ruler aligned with one of the seams. Straighten the edge periodically by trimming a skinny slice if necessary.

SET-IN SEAMS

While many of the Schoolhouse blocks in this book call for simple, straight seam sewing, occasionally the design of a block will require that you

sew a set-in seam. A set-in seam is one that requires you to fit a piece (or pieces) into the quilt block by pivoting at a key point. Although this is not especially difficult, it does call for some advance planning.

The need for a set-in seam can be seen in the roof and skyline of House 2 in **Diagram 3.** While House 1 can be completed by adding Rows 2 and 3 with simple, straight seam sewing, the A and A reverse pieces cannot be added to House 2 quite so simply. Because of the angled seams, you will need to turn a corner to get the pieces to fit.

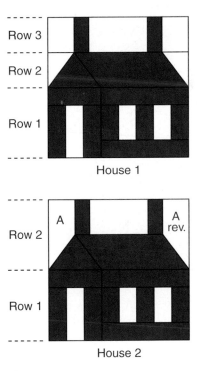
Diagram 3

Step 1. Sew the roof unit to the top of the house, as shown in **Diagram 4.**

Diagram 4

Step 2. Place a fabric A piece along the chimney edge, with right sides together and top edges aligned. Use a pencil to mark a dot ¼ inch from the bottom edge of A, as shown in **Diagram 5A.** Pin, then begin sewing at the dot, taking a ¼-inch seam allowance. Start with a backstitch and stitch outward in the direction indicated by the arrow. Wait to press.

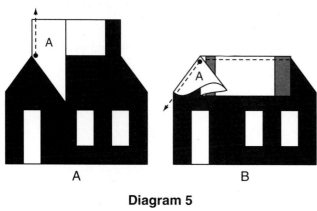

A   B

Diagram 5

Step 3. Manuever the A piece so that its angled bottom edge is aligned with the angled edge of the large pieced unit, as shown in **5B.** Pin, taking care that the marked dot is secured at the pivot point. Once again, begin sewing at the dot, taking a ¼-inch seam allowance. Backstitch, then stitch outward in the direction indicated by the arrow. Finish by pressing both seams away from A.

Step 4. Repeat Steps 1 through 3 to attach the A reverse piece to the opposite side of the block.

While it is generally easier to stitch outward from a pivot point, this is not always possible. The Eclectic Neighborhood on page 14 provides a good example of a quilt requiring you to complete a series of long seams, turning corners as you go.

Begin by marking all of the ¼-inch pivot points before you start to sew. Work from pivot point to pivot point, pinning and taking the standard ¼-inch seam allowance. Adjust your stitching so that you finish with the sewing machine needle in the down position as you reach each pivot point. Pin to the next pivot point, turn the quilt top under the machine needle, and continue sewing. Work your way from point to point until the rows are completely joined.

Sew Easy

While it is advisable to press seam allowances toward the darker of the two sewn fabrics, this is not always possible, especially when set-in seams are involved. You can eliminate the problem of darker seam allowances shadowing through lighter fabrics by carefully grading the seam allowances. Trim the darker allowance to a *scant* ¼ inch (or ³⁄₁₆ inch) so that it hides behind the lighter—and wider—seam allowance.

SET VARIATIONS

The quilts in this book demonstrate a wide variety of setting arrangements for the Schoolhouse block. In some of the quilts, the Schoolhouse block is arranged in a simple side-by-side straight setting. The straight-set vertical and horizontal rows form the entire quilt top, which is then finished with one or more borders.

In other quilts, the Schoolhouse blocks are separated by plain setting squares or sashing (either pieced or unpieced). Sometimes the sashing strips include corner squares at the junctures where sashing strips meet. Like the sashing strips themselves, these corner squares can be either pieced or unpieced. In Row Houses on page 48, the houses are rotated to be mirror images for yet another look.

The Schoolhouse makes a marvelous focal point for a medallion-style quilt, as demonstrated by House Medallion on page 58. Surrounded by a variety of pieced and plain borders, the Schoolhouse block truly becomes the star of the show. As an alternative, the Schoolhouse block can be incorporated as a secondary block in a series of borders or—in miniature size—as the corner square in a sashed quilt.

The idea of scaling down the Schoolhouse and incorporating it into a larger block is demonstrated quite effectively in two quilts in this book. In The Eclectic Neighborhood on page 14, a simplified

Sew Easy

If you prefer an on-point setting for your quilt but don't want sideways house blocks, you can adapt them with the addition of finishing triangles, as shown. To determine what size triangle is needed, use a sheet of graph paper to draw a square the finished size of the School-house block. Cut the triangle in half diagonally in both directions. The resulting quarter-square triangle is the *template* you will need to change the orientation of the block. Add ¼-inch seam allowances to *each* side of the template before using it to cut fabric triangles. Place the template with the short edges on the straight of grain to cut fabric pieces.

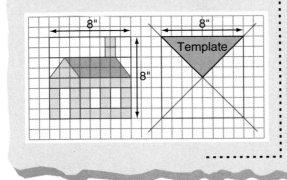

foundation-pieced miniature Schoolhouse is surrounded by four acutely angled triangles for a fresh new look. In My Cabin Made of Logs on page 68, a miniature Schoolhouse becomes the centerpiece for the traditional Log Cabin block. This treatment gives rise to all sorts of design possibilities. Almost any traditional block that includes a large center square can be adapted for a miniature version of the Schoolhouse block.

Teacher of the Year on page 94 presents another possibility for setting the Schoolhouse block. In this quilt, the Schoolhouse is alternated with a series of simple pieced blocks that have been shaded to create an overall barn raising effect. You may wish to experiment with graph paper and pencil to see what other simple setting blocks pair well with the Schoolhouse motif.

PIECING THE QUILT BACKING

Depending upon the size of your quilt, you may not have to piece the quilt back, such as for the small All-American Schoolhouses on page 32, which is less than 36 inches square. However, if you are making a larger wallhanging or a bed-size quilt, piecing the backing is necessary. **Diagram 6** shows how quilt backings are generally pieced together for each quilt size. Refer to the project directions, however, for information on yardage, how to cut the backing fabric, and how to seam it.

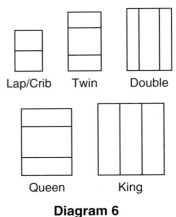

Diagram 6

Sew Quick

If your quilt has a special story, here's a quick and easy way to include the details on a label. Cut a generously sized square (about 6 inches) of muslin or other light-color fabric and another of freezer paper. Using a dry iron, press the waxed side of the freezer paper to the wrong side of the fabric. Then insert the paper-stiffened fabric into a typewriter and type the tale of your quilt! Include information about how and why the quilt was made; note any historic events that took place while you were making it; add a special message for the quilt's recipient. Be sure to include your name and the date. When you are finished, simply remove the paper, finish the raw edges of the fabric as desired, and stitch the completed label to the back of the quilt.

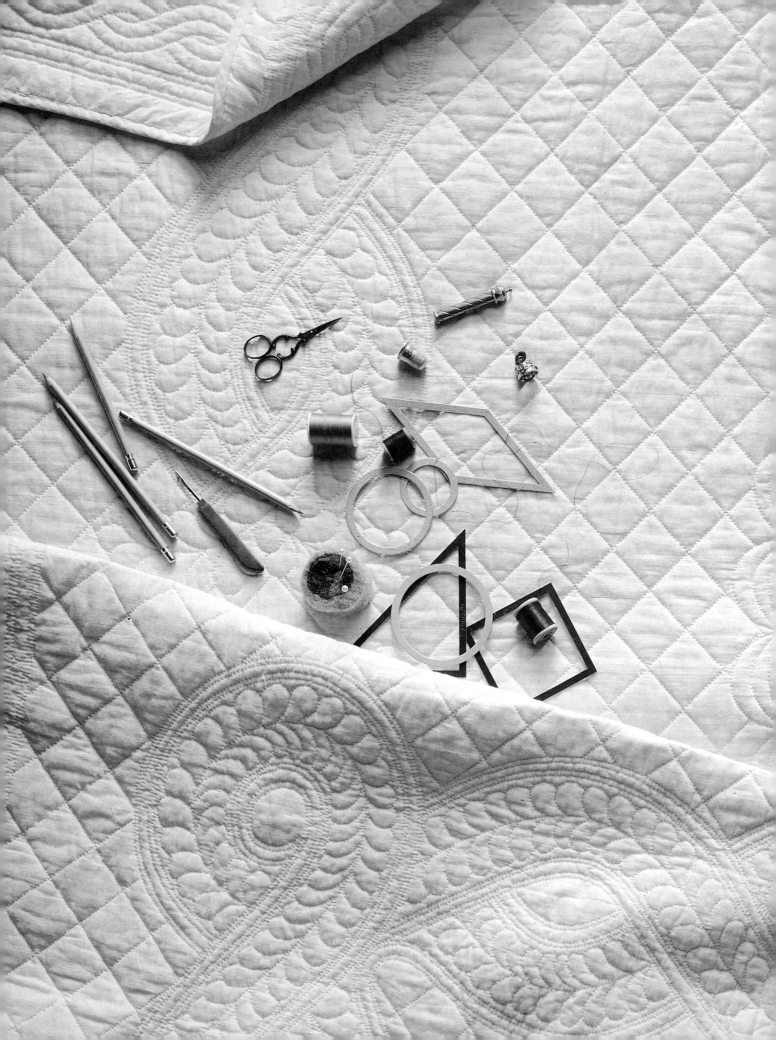

QUILTMAKING
BASICS

This section provides a refresher course in basic quiltmaking techniques. Refer to it as needed; it will help not only with the projects in this book but also with all your quiltmaking.

QUILTMAKER'S BASIC SUPPLY LIST

Here's a list of items you should have on hand before beginning a project.

• **Iron and ironing board:** Make sure these are set up near your sewing machine. Careful pressing leads to accurate piecing.

• **Needles:** The two types of needles commonly used by quilters are *betweens,* short needles used for hand quilting, and *sharps,* long, very thin needles used for appliqué and hand piecing. The thickness of hand-sewing needles decreases as their size designation increases. For instance, a size 12 needle is smaller than a size 10.

• **Rotary cutter, plastic ruler, and cutting mat:** Fabric can be cut quickly and accurately with rotary-cutting equipment. There are a variety of cutters available, all with slightly different handle styles and safety latches. Rigid, see-through acrylic rulers are used with rotary cutters. A 6 × 24-inch ruler is a good size; for the most versatility, be sure it has 45 and 60 degree angle markings. A 14-inch square ruler will also be helpful for making sure blocks are square. Always use a special mat with a rotary cutter. The mat protects the work surface and helps to grip the fabric. Purchase the largest mat practical for your sewing area. A good all-purpose size is 18 × 24 inches.

• **Safety pins:** These are generally used to baste quilts for machine quilting. Use rustproof nickel-plated brass safety pins, preferably in size #0.

• **Scissors:** You'll need several pairs of scissors—shears for cutting fabric, general scissors for cutting paper and template plastic, and small, sharp embroidery scissors for trimming threads.

• **Seam ripper:** A seam ripper with a small, extra-fine blade slips easily under any stitch length.

• **Sewing machine:** Any machine with a straight stitch is suitable for piecing quilt blocks. Follow the manufacturer's recommendations for cleaning and servicing your sewing machine.

• **Straight pins:** Choose long, thin pins with glass or plastic heads that are easy to see against fabric so that you don't forget to remove one.

• **Template material:** Sheets of clear and opaque template plastic can be purchased at most quilt or craft shops. Gridded plastic is also available and may help you to draw shapes more easily. Various weights of cardboard can also be used for templates, including common household items like cereal boxes, poster board, and manila file folders.

• **Thimbles:** For hand quilting, a thimble is almost essential. Look for one that fits the finger you use to push the needle. The thimble should be snug enough to stay put when you shake your hand. There should be a bit of space between the end of your finger and the inside of the thimble.

• **Thread:** For hand or machine piecing, 100 percent cotton thread is a traditional favorite. Cotton-covered polyester is also acceptable. For hand quilting, use 100 percent cotton quilting thread. For machine quilting, you may want to try clear nylon thread as the top thread, with cotton thread in the bobbin.

• **Tweezers:** Keep a pair of tweezers handy for removing bits of thread from ripped-out seams and for pulling away scraps of removable foundations. Regular cosmetic tweezers will work fine.

SELECTING AND PREPARING FABRICS

The traditional fabric choice for quilts is 100 percent cotton. It handles well, is easy to care for, presses easily, and frays less than synthetic blends.

The yardages in this book are generous estimates based on 44/45-inch-wide fabrics. It's a good idea to always purchase a bit more fabric than necessary to compensate for shrinkage and occasional cutting errors.

Prewash your fabrics using warm water and a mild soap or detergent. Test for colorfastness by first soaking a scrap in warm water. If colors bleed, set the dye by soaking the whole piece of fabric in a solution of 3 parts cold water to 1 part vinegar. Rinse the fabric several times in warm water. If it still bleeds, don't use it in a quilt that will need laundering—save it for a wallhanging that won't get a lot of use.

After washing, preshrink your fabric by drying it in a dryer on the medium setting. To keep wrinkles under control, remove the fabric from the dryer while it's still slightly damp and press it immediately with a hot iron.

CUTTING FABRIC

The cutting instructions for each project follow the list of materials. Whenever possible, the instructions are written to take advantage of quick rotary-cutting techniques. In addition, some projects include patterns for those who prefer to make templates and scissor cut individual pieces.

Although rotary cutting can be faster and more accurate than cutting with scissors, it has one disadvantage: It does not always result in the most efficient use of fabric. In some cases, the method results in long strips of leftover fabric. Don't think of these as waste; just add them to your scrap bag for future projects.

Rotary-Cutting Basics

Follow these two safety rules every time you use a rotary cutter: Always cut *away* from yourself, and always slide the blade guard into place as soon as you stop cutting.

Step 1: You can cut several layers of fabric at a time with a rotary cutter. Fold the fabric with the selvage edges together. You can fold it again if you want, doubling the number of layers to be cut.

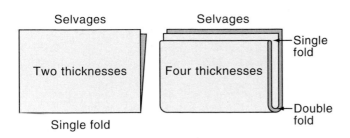

Step 2: To square up the end of the fabric, place a ruled square on the fold and slide a 6 × 24-inch ruler against the side of the square. Hold the ruler in place, remove the square, and cut along the edge of the ruler. If you are left-handed, work from the other end of the fabric.

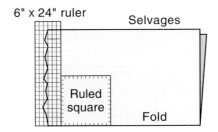

Step 3: For patchwork, cut strips or rectangles on the crosswise grain, then subcut them into smaller pieces as needed. The diagram shows a strip cut into squares.

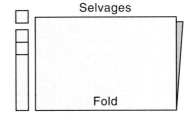

Step 4: A square can be subcut into two triangles by making one diagonal cut (A). Two diagonal cuts yield four triangles (B).

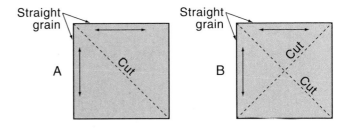

Step 5: Check strips periodically to make sure they're straight and not angled. If they are angled, refold the fabric and square up the edges again.

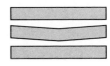

ENLARGING PATTERNS

Every effort has been made to provide full-size pattern pieces. But in some cases, where the pattern piece is too large to fit on the page, only one-half or one-quarter of the pattern is given. Instructions on the pattern piece will tell you where to position the pattern to continue tracing to make a full-size template.

MAKING AND USING TEMPLATES

To make a plastic template, place template plastic over the book page, trace the pattern onto the plastic, and cut out the template. To make a cardboard template, copy the pattern onto tracing paper, glue the paper to the cardboard, and cut out the template. With a permanent marker, record on every template any identification letters and grain lines, as well as the size and name of the block and the number of pieces needed. Always check your templates against the printed pattern for accuracy.

The patchwork patterns in this book are printed with double lines. The inner dashed line is the finished size of the piece, while the outer solid line includes seam allowance.

For hand piecing: Trace the inner line to make finished-size templates. Cut out the templates on the traced line. Draw around the templates on the wrong side of the fabric, leaving ½ inch between pieces. Then mark ¼-inch seam allowances before you cut out the pieces.

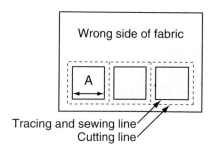

Wrong side of fabric

A

Tracing and sewing line
Cutting line

For machine piecing: Trace the outer solid line on the printed pattern to make templates with seam allowance included. Draw around the templates on the wrong side of the fabric and cut out the pieces on this line.

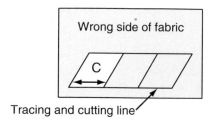

Wrong side of fabric

C

Tracing and cutting line

For appliqué: Appliqué patterns in this book have only a single line and are finished size. Draw around the templates on the right side of the fabric, leaving ½ inch between pieces. Add ⅛- to ¼-inch seam allowances by eye as you cut the pieces.

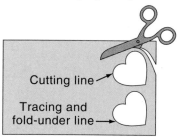

Cutting line

Tracing and
fold-under line

PIECING BASICS

Standard seam allowance for piecing is ¼ inch. Machine sew a sample seam to test the accuracy of the seam allowance; adjust as needed. For hand piecing, the sewing line is marked on the fabric.

Hand Piecing

Cut fabric pieces using finished-size templates. Place the pieces right sides together, match marked seam lines, and pin. Use a running stitch along the marked line, backstitching every four or five stitches and at the beginning and end of the seam.

When you cross seam allowances of previously joined units, leave the seam allowances free. Backstitch just before you cross, slip the needle through the seam allowance, backstitch just after you cross, then resume stitching the seam.

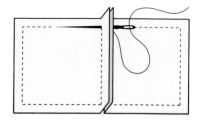

Machine Piecing

Cut the fabric pieces using templates with seam allowances included or using a rotary cutter and ruler without templates. Set the stitch length at 10 to 12 stitches per inch.

Place the fabric pieces right sides together, then sew from raw edge to raw edge. Press seams before crossing them with other seams, pressing toward the darker fabric whenever possible.

Chain piecing: Use this technique when you need to sew more than one of the same type of unit. Place the fabric pieces right sides together and, without lifting the presser foot or cutting the thread, run the pairs through the sewing machine one after another. Once all the units you need have been sewn, snip them apart and press.

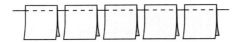

Setting In Pieces

Pattern pieces must sometimes be set into angles created by other pieces, as shown in the diagram. Here, pieces A, B, and C are set into the angles created by the four joined diamond pieces.

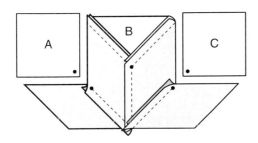

Step 1: Keep the seam allowances open where the piece is to be set in. Begin by sewing the first seam in the usual manner, beginning and ending the seam ¼ inch from the edge of the fabric and backstitching at each end.

Stitch direction →

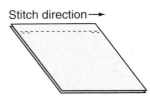

Step 2: Open up the pattern pieces and place the piece to be set in right sides together with one of the first two pieces. Begin the seam ¼ inch from the edge of the fabric and sew to the exact point where the first seam ended, backstitching at the beginning and end of the seam.

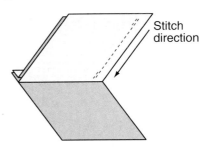

Stitch direction

Step 3: Rotate the pattern pieces so that you are ready to sew the final seam. Keeping the seam allowances free, sew from the point where the last seam ended to ¼ inch from the edge of the piece.

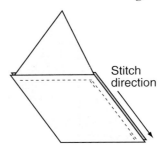

Stitch direction

Step 4: Press the seams so that as many of them as possible lie flat. The finished unit should look like the one shown here.

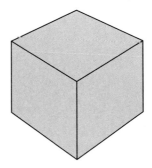

APPLIQUÉ BASICS

Review "Making and Using Templates" to learn how to prepare templates for appliqué. Lightly draw around each template on the right side of the fabric using a pencil or other nonpermanent marker. These are the fold-under lines. Cut out the pieces ⅛ to ¼ inch to the outside of the marked lines.

The Needle-Turn Method

Pin the pieces in position on the background fabric, always working in order from the background to the foreground. For best results, don't turn under or appliqué edges that will be covered by other appliqué pieces. Use a thread color that matches the fabric of the appliqué piece.

Step 1: Bring the needle up from under the appliqué patch exactly on the drawn line. Fold under the seam allowance on the line to neatly encase the knot.

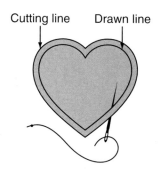

Cutting line   Drawn line

Step 2: Insert the tip of the needle into the background fabric right next to where the thread comes out of the appliqué piece. Bring the needle out of the background fabric approximately ¹⁄₁₆ inch away from and up through the very edge of the fold, completing the first stitch.

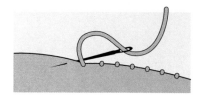

Step 3: Repeat this process for each stitch, using the tip and shank of your appliqué needle to turn under ½-inch-long sections of seam allowance at a time. As you turn under a section, press it flat with your thumb and then stitch it in place, as shown.

PRESSING BASICS

Proper pressing can make a big difference in the appearance of a finished block or quilt top. It allows patchwork to open up to its full size, permits more precise matching of seams, and results in smooth, flat work. Quilters are divided on the issue of whether a steam or dry iron is best; experiment to see which works best for you. Keep these tips in mind:

• Press seam allowances to one side, not open. Whenever possible, press toward the darker fabric. If you find you must press toward a lighter fabric, trim the dark seam allowance slightly to prevent show-through.

• Press seams of adjacent rows of blocks, or rows within blocks, in opposite directions. The pressed seams will fit together snugly, producing precise intersections.

• Press, don't iron. Bring the iron down gently and firmly. This is especially important if you are using steam.

• To press appliqués, lay a towel on the ironing board, turn the piece right side down on the towel, and press very gently on the back side.

ASSEMBLING QUILT TOPS

Lay out all the blocks for your quilt top using the quilt diagram or photo as a guide to placement. Pin and sew the blocks together in vertical or horizontal rows for straight-set quilts and in diagonal rows for diagonal-set quilts. Press the seam allowances in opposite directions from row to row so that the seams will fit together snugly when rows are joined.

To keep a large quilt top manageable, join rows into pairs first and then join the pairs. When pressing a completed quilt top, press on the back side first, carefully clipping and removing hanging threads; then press the front.

MITERING BORDERS

Step 1: Start by measuring the length of your finished quilt top through the center. Add to that figure two times the width of the border, plus 5 inches extra. This is the length you need to cut the two side borders. For example, if the quilt top is 48 inches long and the border is 4 inches wide, you need two borders that are each 61 inches long (48 + 4 + 4 + 5 = 61). In the same manner, calculate the length of the top and bottom borders, then cut the borders.

Step 2: Sew each of the borders to the quilt top, beginning and ending the seams ¼ inch from the edge of the quilt. Press the border seams flat from the right side of the quilt.

Step 3: Working at one corner of the quilt, place one border on top of the adjacent border. Fold the top border under so that it meets the edge of the other border and forms a 45 degree angle, as shown in the diagram. If you are working with a plaid or striped border, check to make sure the stripes match along this folded edge. Press the fold in place.

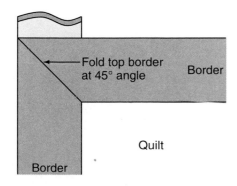

Step 4: Fold the quilt top with right sides together and align the edges of the borders. With the pressed fold as the corner seam line and the body of the quilt out of the way, sew from the inner corner to the outer corner, as shown in the diagram.

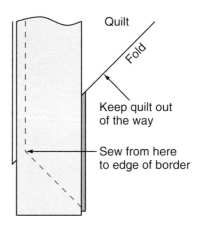

Step 5: Unfold the quilt and check to make sure that all points match and the miter is flat. Trim the border seam allowance to ¼ inch and press the seam open.

Step 6: Repeat Steps 3 through 5 for the three remaining borders.

MARKING QUILTING DESIGNS

To mark a quilting design, use a commercially made stencil, make your own stencil using a sheet of plastic, or trace the design from a book page. Use a nonpermanent marker, such as a silver or white pencil, chalk pencil, or chalk marker, that will be visible on the fabric. You can even mark with a 0.5 mm lead pencil, but be sure to mark lightly.

If you are using a quilt design from this book, either trace the design onto tracing paper or photocopy it. If the pattern will be used many times, glue it to cardboard to make it sturdy.

For light-color fabrics that you can see through, place the pattern under the quilt top and trace the quilting design directly onto the fabric. Mark in a thin, continuous line that will be covered by the quilting thread.

With dark fabrics, mark from the top by drawing around a hard-edged design template. To make a simple template, trace the design onto template plastic and cut it out around the outer edge. Trace around the template onto the fabric, then add inner lines by eye.

LAYERING AND BASTING

Carefully preparing the quilt top, batting, and backing will ensure that the finished quilt will lie flat and smooth. Place the backing wrong side up on a large table or clean floor. Center the batting on the backing and smooth out any wrinkles. Center the quilt top right side up on the batting; smooth it out and remove any loose threads.

If you plan to hand quilt, baste the quilt with thread. Use a long darning needle and white thread. Baste outward from the center of the quilt in a grid of horizontal and vertical rows approximately 4 inches apart.

If you plan to machine quilt, baste with safety pins. Thread basting does not hold the layers securely enough during machine quilting, plus the thread is more difficult to remove when quilting is completed. Use rustproof nickel-plated brass safety pins in size #0, starting in the center of the quilt and pinning approximately every 3 inches.

HAND QUILTING

For best results, use a hoop or a frame to hold the quilt layers taut and smooth during quilting. Work with one hand on top of the quilt and the other hand underneath, guiding the needle. Don't worry about the size of your stitches in the beginning; concentrate on making them even, and they will get smaller over time.

Getting started: Thread a needle with quilting thread and knot the end. Insert the needle through the quilt top and batting about 1 inch away from where you will begin stitching. Bring the needle to the surface in position to make the first stitch. Gently tug on the thread to pop the knot through the quilt top and bury it in the batting.

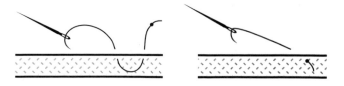

Taking the stitches: Insert the needle through the three layers of the quilt. When you feel the tip of the needle with your underneath finger, gently guide it back up through the quilt. When the needle comes through the top of the quilt, press your thimble on the end with the eye to guide it down again through the quilt layers. Continue to quilt in this manner, taking two or three small running stitches at a time.

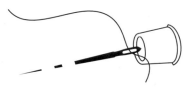

Ending a line of stitching: Bring the needle to the top of the quilt just past the last stitch. Make a knot at the surface by bringing the needle under the thread where it comes out of the fabric and up through the loop of thread it creates. Repeat this knot and insert the needle into the hole where the thread comes out of the fabric. Run the needle inside the batting for an inch and bring it back to the surface. Tug gently on the thread to pop the knot into the batting layer. Clip the thread.

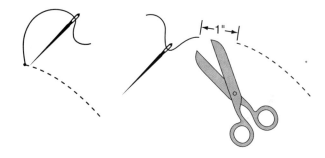

MACHINE QUILTING

For best results when doing machine-guided quilting, use a walking foot (also called an even feed foot) on your sewing machine. For free-motion quilting, use a darning or machine-embroidery foot.

Use thread to match the fabric colors, or use clear nylon thread in the top of the machine and a white or colored thread in the bobbin. To secure the thread at the beginning of a line of stitches, adjust the stitch length on your machine to make several very short stitches, then gradually increase to the regular stitch length. As you near the end of the line, gradually reduce the stitch length so that the last few stitches are very short.

For machine-guided quilting, keep the feed dogs up and move all three layers as smoothly as you can under the needle. To turn a corner in a quilting design, stop with the needle inserted in the fabric, raise the foot, pivot the quilt, lower the foot, and continue stitching.

For free-motion quilting, disengage the feed dogs so you can manipulate the quilt freely as you stitch. Guide the quilt under the needle with both hands, coordinating the speed of the needle with the movement of the quilt to create stitches of consistent length.

MAKING AND ATTACHING BINDING

Double-fold binding, which is also called French-fold binding, can be made from either straight-grain or bias strips. To make double-fold binding, cut strips of fabric four times the finished width of the binding, plus seam allowance. In general, cut strips 2 inches wide for quilts with thin batting or scalloped edges and 2¼ to 2½ inches wide for quilts with thicker batting.

Straight-Grain Binding

To make straight-grain binding, cut crosswise strips from the binding fabric in the desired width. Sew them together end to end with diagonal seams.

Place the strips with right sides together so that each strip is set in ¼ inch from the end of the other strip. Sew a diagonal seam and trim the excess fabric, leaving a ¼-inch seam allowance.

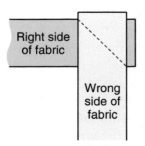

Continuous Bias Binding

Bias binding can be cut in one long strip from a square of fabric that has been cut apart and resewn into a tube. To estimate the number of inches of binding a particular square will produce, use this formula:

Multiply the length of one side by the length of another side, and divide the result by the width of binding you want. Using a 30-inch square and 2¼-inch binding as an example: $30 \times 30 = 900$; $900 \div 2\frac{1}{4} = 400$ inches of binding.

Step 1: To make bias binding, cut a square in half diagonally to get two triangles. Place the two triangles right sides together, as shown, and sew with a ¼-inch seam. Open out the two pieces and press the seam open.

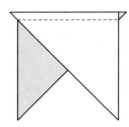

Step 2: Using a pencil and a see-through ruler, mark cutting lines on the wrong side of the fabric in the desired binding width. Draw the lines parallel to the bias edges.

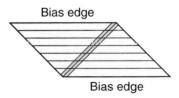

Step 3: Fold the fabric with right sides together, bringing the two nonbias edges together and offsetting them by one strip width (as shown in the diagram at the top of page 122). Pin the edges together, creating a tube, and sew with a ¼-inch seam. Press the seam open.

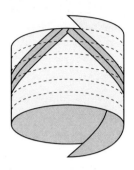

Step 4: Cut on the marked lines, turning the tube to cut one long bias strip.

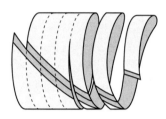

Attaching the Binding

Trim excess batting and backing even with the quilt top. For double-fold binding, fold the long binding strip in half lengthwise, with wrong sides together, and press. Beginning in the middle of a side, not in a corner, place the strip right sides together with the quilt top, align raw edges, and pin.

Step 1: Fold over approximately 1 inch at the beginning of the strip and begin stitching ½ inch from the fold. Sew the binding to the quilt, using a ¼-inch seam and stitching through all layers.

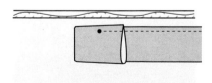

Step 2: As you approach a corner, stop stitching ¼ inch from the raw edge of the corner. Backstitch and remove the quilt from the machine. Fold the binding strip up at a 45 degree angle, as shown in the following diagram on the left. Fold the strip back down so there is a fold at the upper

edge, as shown on the right. Begin sewing ¼ inch from the top edge of the quilt, continuing to the next corner. Miter all four corners in this manner.

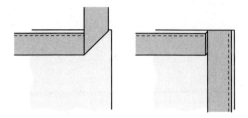

Step 3: To finish the binding seam, overlap the folded-back beginning section with the ending section. Stitch across the fold, allowing the end to extend approximately ½ inch beyond the beginning.

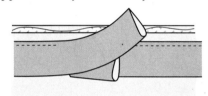

Step 4: Turn the binding to the back of the quilt and blindstitch the folded edge in place, covering the machine stitches with the folded edge. Fold in the adjacent sides on the back and take several stitches in the miter. In the same way, add several stitches to the miters on the front.

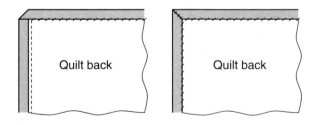

SIGNING YOUR QUILT

Be sure to sign and date your finished quilt. Your finishing touch can be a simple signature in permanent ink or an elaborate inked or embroidered label. Add any other pertinent details that can help family members or quilt collectors 100 years from now understand what went into your labor of love.